British Colours &
Standards 1747–1881 (2)

Infantry

Ian Sumner • Illustrated by Richard Hook

Series editor Martin Windrow

First published in Great Britain in 2001 by Osprey Publishing,
Elms Court, Chapel Way, Botley, Oxford OX2 9LP, United Kingdom.
Email: info@ospreypublishing.com

ISBN 1 84176 201 6

Editor: Martin Windrow
Design: Alan Hamp
Index by Alan Rutter
Drawings by Ian Sumner

Origination by Magnet Harlequin, Uxbridge, UK
Printed in China through World Print Ltd.

01 02 03 04 05   10 9 8 7 6 5 4 3 2 1

FOR A CATALOGUE OF ALL BOOKS PUBLISHED BY
OSPREY MILITARY AND AVIATION PLEASE CONTACT:
The Marketing Manager, Osprey Direct UK, PO Box 140
Wellingborough, Northants, NN8 4ZA, United Kingdom
Email: **info@ospreydirect.co.uk**

The Marketing Manager, Osprey Direct USA
c/o Motorbooks International
PO Box 1, Osceola, WI 54020-0001, USA
Email: **info@ospreydirectusa.com**

www.ospreypublishing.com

Acknowledgements

I would like to thank everyone who has helped with this book: my
wife, Robin Ashburner, Roy Wilson, the staffs of the British Library,
the library of the National Army Museum, the Scottish National War
Museum, and the Regimental Museum of the Sherwood Foresters.

Artist's Note

Readers may care to note that the original paintings from which the
colour plates in this book were prepared are available for private
sale. All reproduction copyright whatsoever is retained by the
Publishers. All enquiries should be addressed to:

Scorpio Gallery, PO Box 475, Hailsham, E.Sussex BN27 2SL, UK

The Publishers regret that they can enter into no correspondence
upon this matter.

Glossary

Colours The large square or oblong flags carried by infantry
regiments.
Corner, first, second, etc. The first corner is that in the top left
corner of the sheet (q.v.), with the staff on the viewer's left; the
second corner is in the top right corner; the third corner in the
bottom left; the fourth corner in the bottom right.
Ferrule A metal shoe fixed to the bottom end of the flagstaff.
Finial The decorative metalwork at the top of each flagstaff. It took
the form of a spearhead until 1855, when it was replaced by the lion
and crown of the Royal crest.
Fly That part of the sheet (q.v.) furthest away from the staff.
Guidon A small swallow-tailed flag carried by regiments of
dragoons.
Hoist That part of the sheet (q.v.) nearest the staff.
Obverse The side of the flag shown when the staff is to the viewer's
left.
Reverse The side of the flag shown when the staff is to the viewer's
right.
Sheet The whole of the cloth of a flag.
Standard A small square or oblong flag carried, in the British Army,
by regiments of horse and dragoon guards.

BRITISH COLOURS & STANDARDS 1747–1881 (2) INFANTRY

THE 1747 REGULATIONS

The 1747 Regulations required that each regiment of Foot carry two colours. One of these was to be the King's, or First, Colour; the other was to be called simply the Second Colour. The King's Colour was to consist of the 'Great Union', that is the Union Flag, throughout. The Second Colour was to be in the colour of the regimental facings, with a small Union Flag in the upper hoist corner (see glossary). An exception was made for the five regiments with facings in white (the 17th, 32nd, 43rd and 47th) or red (the 33rd). These regiments were to carry a Second Colour of white with a red cross 'of St. George', and the Union Flag in the upper hoist corner, as described above. A pure white flag could easily be confused with a flag of surrender, but the objection to a red flag is harder to identify. A plain red flag has since been used in some countries (though not the United Kingdom) to indicate 'no quarter' in an approaching battle. A red Regimental Colour would also have been similar to that carried by the Foot Guards, and the provision may have been included to allow the Guards to maintain their distinctiveness in this area.

The regulations were explicit about the kind of device that could be displayed on the colours. No colonel was 'to put his arms, crest, device or livery on any part of the appointments of the Regiment under his command'. (As well as the regiment's colours, these included such items as the coats and drums of the drummers, and the caps of the grenadiers.) Instead the centre of the colour would display the 'rank of the regiment', that is the regimental number, in Roman numerals, surrounded by a Union wreath of roses and thistles on the same stalk.

Once again, exceptions were made. Thirteen regiments (the 1st to 8th, 18th, 21st, 23rd, 27th and 41st Regiments of Foot) had all been granted special badges, and these were ordered to be displayed in the centre of the colours, with the regimental number placed towards the upper hoist corner. This still contained the Union Flag, while the other three corners all contained a small badge, the same in each corner but different to that in the centre. These badges are dealt with in more detail below. It need only be noted here that almost all of the badges used are associated with the royal house of Hanover, though by no means all of the regiments so honoured bore a 'Royal' title.

The colours of these 13 regiments were illustrated as part of a series of watercolour paintings for, or by, the Adjutant General, Col.Robert Napier. All of the paintings include a white scroll placed either above or below the central badge. The scroll suggests that each regiment was intended to adopt some form of motto. However, only four (for the 2nd,

3rd, 7th and 18th Regiments) are depicted in the Napier series, while the actual text of the regulations records mottoes for just two of these (the 7th and 18th). Despite the official nature of the paintings, the other two regiments still had to apply to have their mottoes re-granted. A similar set of paintings compiled for the cavalry regiments also bore scrolls (see volume 1, Elite 77). But while scrolls continued to be a feature of cavalry standards, they were absent from infantry colours for much of the 18th century.

The 1747 Regulations have nothing to say about the size of the colours, except to record that they were to be of the same dimensions as those carried by the Foot Guards. At the time of the coronation of King James II the colours of the Foot Guards had been enormous – a full 90ins. on the staff by 99ins. long; by 1747, however, their size had been reduced to a slightly more manageable 72ins. by 78 inches.

It would appear that not all regiments immediately exchanged their old colours for replacements produced to conform to the new regulations. The colours of the 25th Foot, for example, which had been presented in 1743, were

Table 1: Badges and distinctions of Infantry Regiments numbered 1st to 29th

1st The Royal cipher within a circlet bearing the motto of the Order of the Thistle (1747), changed to the collar and badge of the Order of the Thistle, on receiving the subsidiary title 'Royal Scots' (1812), in the centre; a crowned thistle, in three corners (1747), placed on a red ground within a circlet of St Andrew (1812, on receiving the subsidiary title 'Royal Scots'); a Sphinx, under the wreath (1802, to commemorate the campaign in Egypt).

2nd The Queen's cipher CARA (for Queen Caroline, the wife of George II) within the Garter, in the centre, with the motto *Pristinae virtutis memor* (Mindful of our ancient valour) (1747); a lamb, in three corners (1747) – it had become a paschal lamb by 1827, with the extra motto *Vel exuviae triumphant* (Even in death triumphant) added in 1841; Sphinx, under the wreath (1802, to commemorate the campaign in Egypt).

3rd A green dragon, in the centre, with the motto *Veteri frondescet honore* (The glory of our fathers lives in us again) (1747); the motto did not appear in the text of the warrant, and was used unofficially on some stands until given official approval in 1890; a rose and crown, in three corners (1747).

4th The Royal cipher and Garter, in the centre (1747); the lion of England, in three corners (1747); possibly granted for service during the Jacobite Rebellion of 1745.

5th St George and the dragon, in the centre (1747), with the motto *Quo fata vocant* (Wherever fate calls) (1825); rose and crown, in three corners (1747).

6th An antelope, collared and with a chain, in the centre (1747); a Tudor rose and crown, in three corners (1747); according to regimental tradition, granted for gallant behaviour at Almanza (1707).

7th A rose within the Garter, in the centre (1747); a white horse, in three corners (1747).

8th A white horse within the Garter, in the centre, with the motto *Nec aspera terrent* (Hardship has no terrors) (1747); the Royal cipher and crown, in three corners (1747); a Sphinx, under the wreath (1802, to commemorate the campaign in Egypt).

9th The figure of Britannia, in the centre (1799); according to regimental tradition, granted for gallantry at Saragossa (1706), but hardly used by the regiment until the 1770s.

10th A Sphinx, under the wreath (1802, to commemorate the campaign in Egypt).

12th A castle and key, with the motto *Montis insignia Calpe* (The badge of Mount Calpe) under the wreath (1836 to commemorate the siege of Gibraltar, 1779–83); the unofficial motto *Stabilis*, borne c.1772.

13th A Sphinx, under the wreath (1802, to commemorate the campaign in Egypt), mural crown and *Jellalabad*, under the wreath (1842, to commemorate the siege).

14th A white horse, in three corners (1873); a Royal tiger and *India*, under the wreath (1838, for services 1807–31).

17th A Royal tiger and *Hindoostan*, under the wreath (1825, for services 1804–23); regimental tradition asserts that its colours at one time bore a laurel wreath to commemorate its bravery at an engagement at Princeton, in January 1777, but the colours carried on that day were subsequently captured at Stoney Point in 1779, and no documentary evidence exists to confirm the story.

18th A harp below a crown, for the subsidiary title 'Royal Irish', in the centre, with the motto *Virtutis Namurcensis praemium* (The rewards of valour at Namur) (1747, to commemorate the siege of Namur in 1695); the arms of Nassau, in three corners (1747); a Chinese dragon, under the wreath (1843, to commemorate the campaign of 1840–42); a Sphinx, under the wreath (1802, to commemorate the campaign in Egypt).

20th A Sphinx, under the wreath (1802, to commemorate the campaign in Egypt).

21st A Thistle within a circlet bearing the motto of the Order of the Thistle, in the centre (1747); the Royal cipher and crown, in three corners (1747).

23rd The Prince of Wales's plumes, in the centre (1747); a sun rising from behind a cloud, 2nd corner (1747); a red dragon, 3rd corner (1747); the Prince of Wales's plumes, 4th corner (1747, changed to a white horse perhaps by 1807, but not authorised until 1835); a Sphinx, under the wreath (1802, to commemorate the campaign in Egypt).

24th A Sphinx, under the wreath (1802, to commemorate the campaign in Egypt).

25th The coat of arms of Edinburgh, in the centre, with the motto *Nisi Dominus frustra* (Except the Lord be with us, we strive in vain) (1832, to commemorate the place where the regiment was raised in 1689); the Royal crest with the motto *In veritate religio confido* (I trust in the truth of my religion), 2nd and 3rd corners (1828); a white horse and the motto *Nec aspera terrent*, 4th corner (1832, on receiving the subsidiary title 'King's Own Borderers'); a Sphinx, under the wreath (1802, to commemorate the campaign in Egypt).

26th A Sphinx, under the wreath towards the hoist (1802, to commemorate the campaign in Egypt); a Chinese dragon, under the wreath towards the fly (1843, to commemorate the campaign of 1840–42).

27th A three-towered castle and the word *Inniskilling*, in the centre (1747); a white horse, in three corners; a Sphinx, under the wreath (1802, to commemorate the campaign in Egypt).

28th A Sphinx, under the wreath (1802, to commemorate the campaign in Egypt).

carried until 1763. Meanwhile, an inspection return for the 33rd Foot, dated 1754, is rather more ambiguous, noting simply that the regiment had 'two colours received in 1745 and two in 1749.' Did the regiment indeed carry four colours, or is this just an historical note?

The 1751 Regulations

The regulations of 1751 were little more than a reprint of the earlier Warrant. Authority to make alterations in the regulations was extended from the king alone to include 'Our Captain-General' – the king's son, the Duke of Cumberland. The change was short-lived, however; the post of captain-general was abolished on Cumberland's resignation in 1757, and the clause was omitted from the next Warrant in 1768.

Another new clause provided for regiments that had a 2nd Battalion. They were to add a 'pile wavy' in the upper hoist corner of the colours carried by that battalion, in order to distinguish its colours from those of the 1st Battalion. The pile wavy was an old device used on colours in the middle of the 17th century. At that time each company of every regiment carried its own distinctive colour, and the pile wavy had been used to distinguish the colour of the Major's Company. Taken from heraldic practice, it consisted of a narrow, wavy wedge or flame shape descending diagonally from the upper hoist corner.

Colours before the 1747 Regulations, II: Huske's Royal Welch Fuzileers, 1745. Two colours of this design were captured at Fontenoy; one, perhaps the Colonel's Colour, had a crimson sheet, and the other was white. The regiment – later the 23rd of Foot – first acquired a Welsh subsidiary title in 1714, when it was known as the Prince of Wales's Regiment of Welsh Fuzileers, which might account for the prominence of the feathers and coronet badge. The white horse in the centre of the Union canton is a common feature of many of the colours and standards of this period. Source: Lawson, *Uniforms of the British Army*, volume 2.

Some inspecting officers made a special note of regiments whose colours complied with regulations; for example, Lt.Gen. Skelton commented of the 51st Foot in April 1756, 'The colours new and according to regulation.' However, notes of this kind remain an exception in this early period. Reporting on a regiment's colours became a formal part of the inspecting officer's duties only in 1770.

Once again, the 1751 Regulations give no indication as to the size of the colours; however, not all were of standard dimensions. An inspection return of 1753 notes that the colours of the 13th Foot were 'of a less size than other regiments.'

The 1768 Regulations

This issue also repeated much that was contained within the previous Warrants, and new provisions were few. One dealt with the case of the four regiments raised since 1751 that had black facings (the 50th, 58th, 64th and 70th). Like their counterparts with white or red facings, these regiments were ordered to adopt colours with a red cross, but on a sheet that was black instead of white. Another new clause recorded that two more regiments – the 42nd and the 60th – had been granted special badges.

The 1768 Regulations were the first to give specific details of size. Colours were ordered to be 72ins. wide by 78ins. long – identical to those carried by the Foot Guards in 1747; so it would seem likely that the

dimensions chosen simply reflected the current state of affairs. The staff was to be 118ins. long, including the finial.

Changes after 1768

Although the devices permitted on the First and Second Colours were described quite specifically, sufficient leeway was left in the wording of the regulations for their appearance to change over time. Colours produced under the 1751 and 1768 Warrants were required only to have the regimental number in the centre, and many colours of the early 1750s bear that number embroidered directly onto the sheet. By 1760, however, fashions and tastes had moved on. The number now often appeared on a gold-edged cartouche, in the form, for example, 'REG^T / XXXIX'. The surrounding wreath also changed in style. Earlier examples were almost circular, with flowers and leaves that were natural in form, growing on winding stalks; by 1770 these wreaths have spread out sideways and look even more naturalistic. However, exceptions to the dominant style can be found at any period – naturally, since colours were made up by local craftsmen at the request of the regimental colonel. The Second Colour of the 103rd Volunteer Hunters, raised in 1760 and disbanded three years later, bears no wreath as such; instead it displays two branches that do not extend more than three-quarters of the way up the central cartouche (see illustration).

The rambling style of wreath disappeared in its turn in the early 1790s, to be replaced by a balanced, symmetrical affair surrounding a shield-shaped cartouche; from the early 19th century the roses it contained were Tudor roses, rather than the garden variety. The cartouche still bore the regimental number, but in reverse order from the pattern which had obtained previously – e.g. 'XXVIII / REG^T'. Regiments mentioned in the 1751 and 1768 Warrants as the bearers of special badges did not have wreaths at all during this period. Their omission from Napier's paintings suggests that it was intended that the badge should replace both the number and the wreath of the other regiments.

In 1784 the first battle honour to be presented to more than one regiment at the same time was awarded to the 12th, 39th, 56th and 58th Regiments. It was to consist of the word 'Gibraltar', to commemorate service at the siege of 1779–83. In 1836 the honour was amended; each regiment was awarded a new badge consisting of a castle and a key, together with the motto *Montis insignia Calpe*. In 1801, more regiments were rewarded for their heroism at the battle of Minden, some 42 years earlier. The

regiments concerned were the 12th, 20th, 23rd, 25th, 37th and 51st. In the following year the proliferation of battle honours began with the award for the campaign of the previous year in Egypt.

In 1799, a distinctive badge – the figure of Britannia – was granted to the 9th Foot. Then in 1801 came two changes of universal application. Following the Act of Union with Ireland, every stand of colours had to be altered. A red saltire (diagonal cross) was added to the Union Flag, and all the Union wreaths had henceforth to include shamrocks. Neither saltire nor shamrock was known as a national symbol in Ireland at the time, although they were thought of as such in England. Both devices had been incorporated into the insignia of the star of the Order of St Patrick in 1783.

During the early 19th century a number of stylistic changes also took place without the authority of official regulation. For example, use of the 'pile wavy' as the mark of a second battalion had fallen into gradual neglect, and it no longer appears to have been included on new colours issued after the beginning of the 19th century. No provision was made for a distinctive badge to be borne by the third or subsequent battalions of a regiment: neither the 3/1st (see Plate F2) nor the 3/14th, for example, bore their battalion number on their colours.

Further changes were introduced after the end of the Napoleonic Wars. The shield or cartouche, no longer to contemporary tastes, was replaced. The regimental number was now in Arabic numerals on a circular crimson ground, which in turn was surrounded by a crimson circlet, bearing the subsidiary title of the regiment. These titles had first

Some company badges of the Grenadier Guards: (a) No.9 Company, a white greyhound with a gold collar; (b) No.10 Company, a gold sun in splendour; (c) No.14 Company, a white falcon with a gold beak, and with gold bells on its feet, within a gold fetterlock; (d) No.19 Company, a silver sword with a gold hilt crossed with a gold sceptre; (e) No.24 Company, a white stag with gold antlers and hooves leaving a gold tower, placed on a gold and blue heraldic wreath. Source: Dawnay, *Standards of the Household Division.*

Table 2: Badges and distinctions of Infantry Regiments numbered 30th to 69th

30th A Sphinx, under the wreath (1802, to commemorate the campaign in Egypt).

33rd The crest of the Duke of Wellington, under the wreath (1853, when given the subsidiary title 'Duke of Wellington's').

34th A laurel wreath, under the wreath (1843, to commemorate the battle of Arroyo dos Molinos).

36th The regiment bore the unofficial motto *Firm* from c.1846, according to regimental tradition borne on the colours from as early as 1773, although it actually commemorates the battle of Lauffeldt in 1747.

39th A castle and key, under the wreath, with the motto *Montis insignia Calpe* (1836, to commemorate the siege of Gibraltar, 1779–83); the motto *Primus in Indis* (First in India) (1836, to commemorate service prior to and during the battle of Plassey).

40th A Sphinx, under the wreath (1802, to commemorate the campaign in Egypt).

41st A rose and thistle conjoined on the same stalk, in the centre (1747); the Prince of Wales's plumes, under the wreath, with the motto *Gwell angau neu chwilydd* (Better death than shame) (1831, on receiving the subsidiary title 'Welsh'); the Royal cipher and crown, in three corners (1747).

42nd The Royal cipher within the Garter above St Andrew, in the centre (certainly by 1768 but possibly in 1758, when the regiment was granted the subsidiary title 'Royal Highland'); the Royal cipher, in three corners (by 1768); a Sphinx, under the wreath (1802, to commemorate the campaign in Egypt).

44th A Sphinx, under the wreath (1802, to commemorate the campaign in Egypt).

49th A Chinese dragon, under the wreath (1843, to commemorate the campaign of 1840–42).

50th A Sphinx, under the wreath (1802, to commemorate the campaign in Egypt); the Duke of Clarence's cipher, on receiving the subsidiary title 'Duke of Clarence's' (1828), removed on becoming 'Queen's Own' (1831), but no alteration was made to the then current colours.

54th A Sphinx, under the wreath (1802, to commemorate the campaign in Egypt).

55th A Chinese dragon, under the wreath (1843, to commemorate the campaign of 1840–42).

56th A castle and key, under the wreath, with the motto *Montis insignia Calpe* (1836, to commemorate the siege of Gibraltar, 1779–83).

58th A castle and key, under the wreath towards the hoist, with the motto *Montis insignia Calpe* (1836, to commemorate the siege of Gibraltar, 1779–83); a Sphinx, under the wreath towards the fly (1802, to commemorate the campaign in Egypt).

60th The Royal cipher within the Garter, in the centre; the Royal cipher in three corners (1757, on receiving the subsidiary title 'Royal American').

61st A Sphinx, under the wreath (1802, to commemorate the campaign in Egypt).

65th A Royal tiger and *India*, under the wreath (1823, for services 1802–22).

67th A Royal tiger and *India*, under the wreath (1827, for services 1805–26).

68th The regiment used the unofficial motto *Faithful* on the stand carried from 1773, granted according to regimental tradition for services in the West Indies. The stand no longer exists, and there is no documentary evidence to confirm the story.

Colonel's Colour, 2nd Foot Guards, carried by the 2nd Battalion at Waterloo alongside the Colour illustrated Plate A. Issued in 1807, they were later altered by the addition of the battle honours, PENINSULAR and WATERLOO in 1815–16. Sheet: crimson. Lettering: gold. Star: silver with a blue Garter lettered in gold, the centre white with a red cross. Sphinx: silver, within a green wreath. Source: Dawnay, *Standards of the Household Division*.

been introduced in 1782 to improve recruiting and usually consisted of a county name. Regiments which lacked such a title – generally the higher numbered regiments raised during the recent wars – omitted the circlet, and the crimson centre extended as far as the wreath. In general, the badge for Egypt was placed immediately below the wreath. The battle honours were placed on scrolls, which at first were light blue with gold edges and lettering, but were later in yellow with black lettering.

None of these changes – the abandonment of the pile wavy, or the alterations to the centre of the colour – was ever prescribed by regulation. They seem instead to have occurred by some kind of informal agreement. In the same way Arabic numbers were abandoned in their turn around 1839 and Roman numerals restored in their place.

The way in which regiments applied for new colours also saw some formal modification. From the 1837 issue of the King's Regulations, all such applications had to be made in the first instance to the Inspector of Regimental Colours. The application was normally made by the regimental Agent on behalf of the Colonel. This was a codification of the practice that had obtained since 1806, although nothing had ever appeared in regulations in the intervening period.

The 1844 Regulations

The 1844 Regulations saw the renaming of both the King's and the Second Colour. The former was retitled the 'Royal Colour' (the term 'Queen's Colour' was not sanctioned until 1892), while the latter finally received official recognition as the 'Regimental Colour', a term that had been in common use since the 18th century.

The Warrant also regularised another area of common practice concerning regimental names. Although a number of regiments had begun informally to add their subsidiary titles to their colours in the years following the end of Napoleonic Wars, this had never been given official approval. In 1844, the Warrant finally provided that: 'Those Regiments which bear a Royal, County or other Title are to have such designation on a red ground round a circle within the Union wreath of Roses, Thistles and

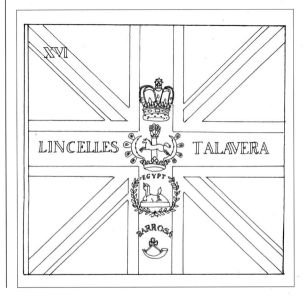

Some company badges of the Coldstream Guards: (a) No.1 Company, a white lion on a green mound; (b) No.3 Company, a white heraldic panther, covered in black, blue and red spots, with yellow and red flames coming from its ears and mouth, standing on a green mound; (c) No.9 Company, a gold knot within a garter of the Order of the Garter, blue with gold edges and lettering; (d) No.10 Company, a gold escarbuncle; (e) No.11 Company, a white boar with gold tusks, hooves and bristles, on a green mound. Source: Dawnay, *Standards of the Household Division*.

Shamrocks. The Number of the Regiment in Gold Roman characters in the centre.' Once more, it is clear that official regulations could do no more than keep pace with stylistic changes rather than dictate them.

A further innovation concerned the display of distinctive badges and battle honours. These had been borne on both the First and the Second Colour for almost a century, but the 1844 Regulations ordered that all devices, distinctions and battle honours were henceforth to be displayed on the Regimental Colour only. This left the Royal Colour with a very austere appearance, with nothing more than a crown and the regimental number in the centre of the Union Flag.

The 1858 Regulations

The 1858 Regulations abolished the spearhead finial, substituting a replacement that depicted the Royal crest of a lion standing upon a crown.

From 1857, colonels ceased to be responsible for the provision of colours to their regiment. Instead, the colours were to be provided via the Army Clothing Department. Since colours were being produced from a central source they adopted a more uniform appearance, particularly as far as the Union wreaths were concerned.

The size of infantry colours was slowly decreasing in the middle years of the 19th century. In 1855 they were reduced by six inches in each dimension. Three years later, on 11 May 1858, they were cut again, more severely this time, to 42ins. wide by 48ins. long. However, the new regulation came in too late to affect the two dozen new stands of colours presented that same year to the recently raised second battalions of the senior regiments, and these over-sized flags continued in service for a number of years to come. The use of the pile wavy to designate a second battalion had long since been abandoned, and on these flags they were now distinguished by a more prosaic scroll under the wreath inscribed 'II Batt.'

The 1868 Regulations

The reduction in the size of the colours soon attracted unfavourable comment, and a remedy was quickly sought. On 5 July 1859, Horse Guards wrote to the Inspector of Regimental Colours: 'The new pattern Colours for the Infantry having, from their reduced size, a poor effect on Parade, I am directed by the General Commanding in Chief to intimate to you that her Majesty has been pleased to sanction the addition of a silk and gold fringe of the pattern sent herewith. The Border for the Queen's Colour [*sic*] is to be of Crimson silk and gold, and that for the Regimental Colour of the Facings of the Corps and gold.' The letter gives no indication of the length of the proposed fringe, although the Queen's Regulations of 1873 specify two inches.

Less than a decade later, however, the 'poor appearance' of the smaller colours no longer seemed to be at issue, for the 1868 edition of the Queen's Regulations reduced their size yet further, to a mere 36ins. wide by 45ins. long.

The 1873 Regulations

The 1873 Regulations included two new provisions, specifying the length of the fringe, as mentioned above, and reducing the size of the staff from a length of 118ins., as stipulated in 1768, to one of 105ins., including the finial.

The 1881 reforms

In the late 1870s the government introduced a number of reforms designed to modernise the organisation and functioning of the Army, named after Edward Cardwell, the Secretary of State for War from 1868 to 1874. The last of these changes were introduced in 1881, but only their effect on infantry colours is considered here. Under the new arrangements, existing regiments were paired to form new regiments, two battalions strong, no longer to be known by a number but by a county name. 'Royal' regiments were to retain their blue facings; other regiments raised in England were to have white facings, Scottish regiments yellow facings and Irish regiments green facings. The full list of battle honours awarded to each of the regiments making up the new unit was to be emblazoned on both of its new Regimental Colours. The

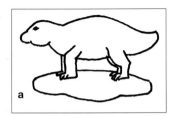

a

b

Table 3: Badges and distinctions of Infantry Regiments numbered 70th and above

72nd (raised 1778) The Duke of York and Albany's cipher and coronet, in three corners (1823, on receiving the subsidiary title 'Duke of Albany's').

73rd (raised 1786) In 1786 at least, used the badge of the Order of the Thistle, perhaps as some kind of carry-over from its previous existence as the 2/42nd.

74th (raised 1787) An elephant and *Assaye*, under the wreath (1807).

75th (raised 1787) A Royal tiger and *India*, under the wreath (1807, for services 1791–1806).

76th (raised 1787) An elephant and *Hindoostan*, under the wreath (1807).

77th (raised 1787) The Prince of Wales's plumes, in the centre, granted for services in India 1787–1807 (1810, although the regiment claimed to have been using the badge for some time before that date); Duke of Cambridge's coronet and cipher (1876, on receiving the subsidiary title 'Duke of Cambridge's').

78th (raised 1793) An elephant and *Assaye*, under the wreath (1807); the motto *Cuidich'n righ* (Help the King) (officially granted 1825, but certainly in use by the regiment's 2nd Battalion as early as 1804 – a motto of the Mackenzie family, one of whom raised the regiment).

79th (raised 1793) A Sphinx, under the wreath (1802, to commemorate the campaign in Egypt).

80th (raised 1793) A Sphinx, under the wreath (1802, to commemorate the campaign in Egypt).

82nd (raised 1793) The Prince of Wales's plumes, in the centre (1831, after receiving the subsidiary title 'Prince of Wales's Volunteers' in 1793).

84th (raised 1775) A thistle within a circlet bearing the motto *Nemo me impune lacessit*, associated with its subsidiary title of 'Royal Highland Emigrants'.

84th (raised 1793) A Union rose, in the centre (1820, after receiving the subsidiary title 'York and Lancaster' in 1809).

85th (raised 1793) The Duke of York's cipher, with the motto *Aucto splendore resurgo* (I rise again with increased splendour) (1815, on receiving the subsidiary title 'Duke of York's', possibly as a reward for services in the Peninsula; the motto ordered discontinued in 1827, when the subsidiary title changed to 'Bucks Volunteers', but resumed 1839).

86th (raised 1793) A harp and crown, in three corners (1812, on receiving the subsidiary title 'Royal County Down'), with the motto *Quis seperabit* (Who shall separate us?) (1832); Sphinx, under the wreath (1802, to commemorate the campaign in Egypt).

87th (raised 1793) The Prince of Wales's plumes, the eagle and laurel wreath, the harp and crown, in the centre, the one above the other (1811, to commemorate the capturing of the eagle of the French 8e *régiment de ligne* at the battle of Barrosa, and on receiving the subsidiary title 'Prince of Wales's').

88th (raised 1793) A harp and crown, in the centre, with the motto *Quis seperabit* (1830); a Sphinx, under the wreath (1802, to commemorate the campaign in Egypt).

89th (raised 1793) The coronet of Princess Victoria in the centre (1866, on receiving the subsidiary title 'Princess Victoria's'); a Sphinx, under the wreath (1802, to commemorate the campaign in Egypt).

90th (raised 1794) A Sphinx, under the wreath (1802, to commemorate the campaign in Egypt).

91st (raised 1794) A boar's head (1873, on receiving the subsidiary title 'Princess Louise's'; a badge of the Campbell Dukes of Argyll – Princess Louise was Duchess); a Sphinx, under the wreath (1802, to commemorate the campaign in Egypt).

92nd When this regiment was ranked 100th, between 1794 and 1798, its colours bore the star of the Order of the Thistle, but this does not appear to have been repeated on later stands.

94th (formed 1793, disbanded 1818) A thistle within a circlet of the Order of the Thistle (1794 stand); the coat of arms of the city of Edinburgh (1812 stand); an elephant, below the wreath (1807).

97th (raised 1826) The motto *Quo fas et gloria ducunt* (Wherever fate and glory lead) (1826, but subsequent use uncertain).

98th (raised 1824) A Chinese dragon, under the wreath (1843, to commemorate the campaign of 1840–42).

99th (raised 1780, disbanded 1784) An alligator (1780, on receiving the subsidiary title 'Jamaica').

99th (raised 1824) The cipher and coronet of the Duke of Edinburgh (1874, on receiving the subsidiary title 'Duke of Edinburgh's').

100th (raised 1855) The Prince of Wales's plumes, in the centre; a maple leaf, in three corners (1855, on receiving the subsidiary title 'Prince of Wales's Royal Canadian').

102nd A Royal tiger, under the wreath (1841, for services during the Third Mysore War).

103rd A Royal tiger, under the wreath towards the hoist (1841, for services at the battles of Plassey and Buxar); an elephant, under the wreath towards the fly (1807, to commemorate the battle of Seringapatam).

105th The motto *Cede nullis* (Give way to no-one), borne when an HEIC regiment, but not repeated on the first stand after transfer to Crown service, presented in 1868.

a   b   c   d   e

**Signs of the times: company badges of the 3rd Foot Guards/ Scots (Fusilier) Guards. Although the written descriptions of these badges did not change during this period, the way in which they were depicted did.
(a) Colonel's Colour, red lion and border on gold, with the round shield of c.1746. (b) No.11 Company, white saltire on blue, shows that by 1793 the shield had become much more elongated. (c) No.6 Company, a blue griffin with red claws and beak on a gold shield, of the 1811 issue; the shield was now much more angular in style. This remained the fashion for some years to come, although the motto scroll became shorter, as in (d) No.1 Company, a red lion and gold crown, carried by the 1st Battalion at the Alma – see commentary to Plate B2. The 1856 issue saw a much more rounded shield, as in (e), the Colonel's Colour. Source: Dawnay, *Standards of the Household Division*.**

first stand of colours under the Cardwell reforms was issued to the 1st Battalion, East Yorkshire Regiment, and taken into use in December 1882. However, some 36 battalions managed to avoid the impact of Cardwell's restructuring by retaining their old colours. For example, the 1st Battalion, Essex Regiment continued to carry the 1857 colours of the 44th Foot for the next hundred years.

An end to Colours in the field

The disaster that overtook the 1/24th Foot at Isandlwana in January 1879, which was only emphasised by the efforts of Lts. Melvill and Coghill to save the Queen's Colour from capture, prompted some discussion of the role of colours in battle. Sir Alexander Gordon MP raised the question in the House of Commons, taking the view that the line infantry should be treated in the same way as the Rifle regiments, which did not carry colours. On 12 August 1880 he enquired whether the Secretary of State for War, Hugh Childers, would 'consider the propriety of discontinuing the antiquated institution of "Colours of a Regiment", and thus place regiments clothed in red on a similar footing to those clothed in green?'

Childers began by consulting with general officers and regimental colonels. However, the argument was given renewed impetus following the British defeat at the hands of the Boers at Laing's Nek on 28 January 1881. The lieutenant carrying the colour of the 58th was killed; and another officer won the Victoria Cross for his attempt to carry him to safety whilst under fire. In the House of Commons, Sir Alexander

The centre of the Second Colour of the 103rd Foot (Volunteer Hunters). The regiment was raised in 1760, and disbanded three years later. Sheet: green. Cartouche: crimson, with the border in two shades of yellow. Note the short but richly embroidered wreath. Source: Milne, *Standards and Colours.*

RIGHT **The centre of the King's Colour, 55th Foot, 1786. Although the wreath is now symmetrical, it still contains natural rather than Tudor roses. Source: Milne, *Standards and Colours.***

FAR RIGHT **The centre of the Second Colour, 39th Foot, c.1786. Sheet: willow green. This is the earliest known representation of a battle honour, but since the Union wreath has been replaced by decorative scrollwork and sprigs of laurel it is impossible to say how typical this display might be. Source: Milne, *Standards and Colours.***

returned to the offensive. The following month he asked once more if the Secretary of State had considered 'discontinuing the use of such impedimenta' as regimental colours; a second MP, Admiral Egerton, also questioned the loss of life that resulted from carrying colours in action; and on 29 July 1881, after further deliberation, Childers made the following statement to the House of Commons:

'In consequence of the altered formation of attack and the extended range of fire, Regimental Colours shall not in future be taken with the battalions on active service. When, however, a battalion goes abroad in the ordinary course of relief, they will accompany the battalion, but be left with the depot which has to be formed on such occasions as the regiment goes on active service. Except in this respect no change will be made, both Colours being retained as affording a record of the services of the regiment and furnishing to the young soldier a history of its gallant deeds. At reviews and occasions of ceremony, they will be usually taken with the battalion.'

The text of this statement formed the basis of a Horse Guards letter sent to all regiments on 17 January 1882. The colours carried by the 58th at Laing's Nek were thus the last to be carried in action by a British regiment. The last colours to be taken on active service were those of the 1st Battalion, South Staffordshire Regiment at Alexandria in 1882.

COLOURS ON SERVICE

Supply and costs

Colours were supplied to infantry regiments in the same way as their cavalry counterparts. The colonel of each regiment was responsible for providing the colours until 1857, when the War Office assumed that duty.

The earliest colours had been embroidered, although as the 18th century progressed painted colours became more common. Painted

colours were certainly much lighter to carry; a stand made during the last decade of the 18th century for the 7th Fusiliers was embroidered so heavily by the royal princesses (their brother, the Duke of Kent, was the colonel of the 7th) that it would hardly fly. On the other hand, painted colours were less durable; they did not last as long when carried in the field, partly because the paint would flake off and partly because of its damaging effect on the silk. The colours of the 30th Foot at Secunderabad in 1825 were described as 'in bad condition, the paint having destroyed the silk'; in the same year those of the 95th were in no better state, 'only three years in use, much injured from the circumstance of the arms and ornaments being painted.' These considerations saw a return to embroidered colours from the 1820s onwards. Perhaps the last painted colours in service were those of the 63rd, issued in 1826 and retired in 1842.

The costs incurred by the colonel in providing colours were considerable. In July 1800 a new stand of colours was ordered for the 72nd Highlanders from Mr Robert Horne of the Barbican, London, at a cost of £26 14s 4d. The timing of the order was unfortunate: within six months, a further £8 8s was needed to make the alterations required following the Union with Ireland. It is likely that these prices reflect the cost of a painted set, for a new stand for the 2nd Battalion of the same regiment, which was ordered in 1804 and is known to have been painted, cost almost exactly the same amount (£26 15s).

Embroidery was the more expensive process. In 1831 a stand of colours for the 47th Foot, again ordered from Horne, cost £40; tassels were extra and cost a further £4 for the two pairs. Part of the increase in price can be attributed to inflation, but in addition, the 47th's colours were almost certainly embroidered. Another stand obtained for the 72nd in 1825, on this occasion from Horne's son, Frederick, was similarly priced at £44 10s.

The pierced spearhead finial remained the standard pattern until the regulations of 1858 introduced the Royal crest. Even so, at least one regiment, the 80th Foot, carried something different. The 80th

The Second Colour of the 102nd Foot, 1794, with the heart-shaped shield typical of the period in the centre, but a most atypical use of Arabic numerals. Sheet: Yellow. Source: actual flag. (Photo National Army Museum 8168)

returned from India in 1814, and a new stand of colours was made and presented while the regiment was in France on occupation duties. 'The colours', recorded an inspecting officer in October of that year, 'were received from England about two months ago; there is a silver sphinx on the top of each staff, which are so heavy that those who carry them are under the necessity of unscrewing them when the regiment begins to move.' In the following year the sphinxes are described as 'gilt and too heavy', and in 1816 as 'very handsome, but too heavy'. The colonel of the regiment took the hint, and no more is heard of them after that date. Milne notes that the sphinxes remained in the Armoury on Malta after the colours were retired in 1827, but describes them as brass.

Condition & longevity

The expected life of a stand of colours in the line infantry long remained unregulated, although in the Guards colours were regularly replaced every seven years. Since the cost fell to the colonel, it was up to him to decide when new colours were purchased. Those of the 51st Foot, presented in 1756, were still in use in 1782, even though they had been described as 'old and ragged from service' as long ago as 1775. The 51st were by no means the only regiment to retain their colours until they were unrecognisable. In 1798 the colours of the 9th were described as 'nothing but rags, so that no device or number could be seen on them'; in 1784 those of the 42nd, although in service for only ten years, were 'totally worn out'; whilst in 1785 those of the 50th, only eight years old, were 'so bad that there scarce remains more than the poles.'

Eventually the War Office ruled that, under normal circumstances and if the regiment was on home service, a stand of colours should last

The centre of the Second Colour of the 116th Highlanders, 1794. The regiment had a very short existence: raised in 1794, its men were drafted into the 42nd in the following year. Sheet: white, but note that contrary to regulations there is no red cross. Source: Tullibardine, Marchioness of, *A Military History of Perthshire* (Perth, 1908).

for 20 years. This was, of course, a minimum: there are several instances of the same colours being carried for a hundred years. The 1st Bn, 2nd Foot was presented with a stand of colours on 10 July 1847 and carried them until 10 July 1947. Similarly, a stand presented to the 58th Foot/2nd Bn, Northamptonshire Regiment was carried between 1860 and 1960, whilst a stand presented in 1857 to the 44th Foot (later the 1st Bn, Essex Regiment) was still in use in 1957. Such longevity was, of course, made possible only by the decision taken in 1881 to end the carrying of colours in the field.

Consecration

In 1830 the Bishop of Jamaica wrote to Lord Hill, the Commander-in-Chief, to ask if there existed any prescribed form of service for the consecration of colours. The reply came back in the negative: 'It is unknown in our Discipline', wrote his Lordship. Yet this was not strictly the case. It is probably true to say that no official form of service had ever been prescribed by Horse Guards. However, on the presentation of colours to the 85th Foot (Royal Volunteers) in 1759 the Rev Rowland Chambre had preached a sermon on the subject of 'Religion the Principle and Support of Rational Courage'; and some kind of consecration ceremony was certainly a feature of these occasions during the Napoleonic Wars.

In 1808 a stand of colours was presented to the 76th Foot and, according to regimental records, was consecrated 'in the usual manner'. Nothing more is said about the service itself, but this form of words indicates that there was at least some sort of set procedure. That this was so is further suggested by the work of the Rev William Pratt of Jonesborough, Co. Armagh. In the same year, he published a book entitled *Divine Service for Camp or Garrison*, no doubt for the benefit of other clerics, which included a 'Sketch of the Form of Consecration of a Stand of Colours'.

There could be a long delay between receipt of a new stand of colours and its formal presentation, perhaps because without an official form of service it could prove difficult to find anyone able to conduct the ceremony. During an inspection of the 96th Foot in 1825, the inspecting officer found that the colours had been taken into service without being consecrated. He had the service 'performed with all due solemnity,' adding, 'I did not omit anything that might contribute to make it properly impressive in the minds of young soldiers. I have reason to expect some good effects from this incident.'

Even after the prompting of the Bishop of Jamaica, official instructions remained vague and confusing. In March 1843 the Adjutant General sent out a letter allowing colours to be taken into use without a formal presentation and religious service. Consecration is only mentioned for the first time in the Queen's Regulations of 1867, and no detailed form of service was officially prescribed until 1899 for the infantry (and 1928 for the cavalry).

a

b

c

d

Colour bearers and guards

As with standards in the cavalry, so colours in the infantry were entrusted to the most junior officers of the regiment. In the eyes of some senior officers this was highly unsatisfactory. Sir John Moore, writing to the Adjutant-General in 1803 about a proposed change in drill movements, stated: 'The objection to trust so important a charge as the direction of the march in line to the Ensigns, is that in our service they are the youngest, least experienced and most giddy officers of the regiment; and our colours are so large and unwieldy that it is next to impossible to carry them upright or steady.' Just how unwieldy was brought home to Ensign Cooke of the 43rd Light Infantry at a field day in 1806; the 15-year-old officer was blown to the ground, 'colours and all', when a gust of wind caught the sheet.

However, while the cavalry took steps to replace these young men in their duty with 'steady' non-commissioned officers, infantry regiments do not seem to have followed suit. Instead, an order of 27 July 1813 authorised the selection of one sergeant per company to be appointed as Colour Sergeant, 'to attend the colours in the field.' Sergeants were armed with spontoons, so they may have been able to play some part in defending the colours and the ensigns. However, since this appointment

The centres of the King's (a) and Second (b) Colours of the 12th Foot, presented in 1804. Note the confident, if not arrogant '&c' below the GIBRALTAR scroll in the centre of the Second Colour: the regiment had also served in the Low Countries, the West Indies and at Seringapatam. Milne sniffs at this as 'an addition which might have been dispensed with.' Sheet: yellow. Sources: Milne, *Standards and Colours*; Monier-Williams, H.B., *The Story of the Colours* (Bury St. Edmunds, 1953?).

was also made in Rifle regiments, which did not carry colours, it must be viewed more as a reward for distinguished service.

Attending the colours in the field was extremely dangerous. Their prominence in the centre of a regiment in line was a convenient aiming mark for the enemy artillery. At Waterloo, 14 sergeants of the 40th were killed or wounded when taking their post around the colours. 'Although I was used to warfare as much as any', wrote Sgt.William Laurence of the moment when he was ordered to take his place with the colours, '[this] was a job I did not at all like, but still I went as boldly to work as I could.' At Chilianwallah the entire colour party of the 24th was wiped out, and the centre companies virtually annihilated; the Regimental Colour was rescued by a private of the regiment, although the Royal Colour was lost.

As the range of small arms increased so did the risk. At the Alma four different officers carried the colours of the 20th Foot. The 21st Fusiliers fared little better, for no less than three officers and 17 sergeants were killed or wounded while attending the colours; and NCOs carried the colours of both the 7th Foot and the 23rd Fusiliers for much of the afternoon, because the officers had been killed.

The loss of a colour was keenly felt by the regiment affected. The 2/69th Foot lost its King's Colour at Quatre Bras, when it was caught in line while trying to withdraw across a field of rye by French cuirassiers. So stung was the regiment by its loss that the regimental tailors were set to work to manufacture a replica. The news of what had really happened

The centres of the King's (a) and Second (b) Colours of the 52nd Foot, 1807. The inclusion of the Royal cipher in the centre of the King's Colour is unauthorised by regulation, but found quite frequently at this period. These colours were presented in 1799 when the regiment returned from India, but the 52nd claimed not to know why, or by whom, the deviation had been authorised (though presumably by the colonel of the regiment, Gen.Trapaud). Source: Milne, *Standards and Colours*.

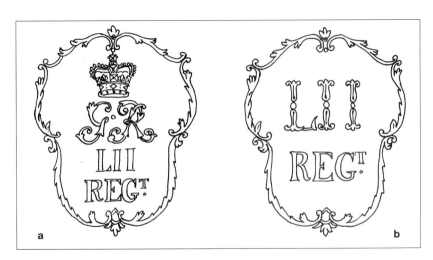

soon spread, however, after the colour was sent to Paris in triumph by Napoleon. The battalion thus found itself in trouble once more for its efforts to conceal its loss. 'Though it is unfortunate in a regiment to lose its colours', thought Sgt. Thomas Morris of the 73rd, a regiment in the same brigade, 'if taken while they are contending with a vastly superior force, as was the case in this instance, it cannot reflect any disgrace on the men.'

Other regiments sought to protect themselves against disaster of this kind. At Buenos Aires in 1807 the colonel of the 88th Foot ordered the colours to be left back at headquarters, fearing that a proposed attack would go badly. In Spain, at the battle of Fuentes d'Onoro, the colonel of the 51st ordered the regiment's colours to be burnt when he thought they were in danger of being captured. As it turned out his assumption was incorrect, and the regiment had to serve for the rest of the campaign without any colours at all. At Waterloo, the colours of the 2/30th and 2/73rd Regiments of Foot were both sent to the rear, out of danger. 'This measure, recalled Maj. McCready of the 30th, 'has been reprobated by many, but I know I never in my life felt such joy or looked on danger with so light a heart, as when I saw our dear old rags in safety. Our brigade [i.e. Halkett's Brigade of Alten's Division – consisting of the 2/30th, 33rd, 2/69th and 2/73rd] did not stand 800 men, and how could they be expected to protect four stands of colours from the most dreaded troops in Europe, approaching with an awful superiority of numbers.'

Similar measures were taken during the Crimean War. At the battle of the Alma the colours of the 21st Fusiliers and those of the 63rd were taken out of the firing line towards a place of safety. This was not necessarily because they were in danger of capture by a Russian counter-attack, but simply because of the number of men killed and wounded in their vicinity. At the siege of Delhi during the Indian Mutiny, the colours of the 61st were removed from their staffs and placed in the Paymaster's chest, while the staffs themselves and the cases were fastened

LEFT **The centre of the Second Colour, 10th Foot, c.1808. Sheet: yellow. Cartouche: red with yellow lettering and edging. Sphinx: silver on a blue disc, within a green wreath, and attached to the main wreath by a crimson ribbon. The circular centre is a forerunner of things to come, but the rambling style of the wreath recalls those of the 1770s. Source: Milne, *Standards and Colours*.**

RIGHT **The centre of the Second Colour of the 2/57th Foot, 1804. The addition of the battalion number to the centre was an unusual feature. The shape of the central cartouche is one that enjoyed a brief period of popularity at the beginning of the 19th century, and was also borne by, amongst others, the 71st. Source: Milne, *Standards and Colours*.**

to the centre poles of the Quarter Guard tent. When the city had finally fallen the colours were retrieved and once more attached to the staffs.

Laying up the Colours

Whilst regiments so clearly honoured their own colours, the War Office could take a much more pragmatic approach. In 1850 the 55th (Westmoreland) Regiment wished to hang its old colours in the parish church in Kendal, the county town. To ensure the safe arrival of these precious items, permission was requested to send them under escort for safekeeping. This was, the War Office thundered, an unnecessary expense: if the church authorities wanted the colours, the Commander-in-Chief could have no objection, but they should be sent in the most economical manner 'for such packages'. It was desirable, the letter continued, to prohibit the employment of Her Majesty's officers and troops in this or any other such 'ridiculous' fashion.

This custom of depositing old colours in a parish or garrison church was, however, uncommon until the third quarter of the 19th century, when stronger links developed between a regiment and the area from which it drew its recruits. However, not everyone was happy to see retired colours deposited in this way. In 1849 the colonel of the 12th (East Suffolk) Foot wished to place the old colours of the 1st Battalion (presented in 1827) in the church of St Mary le Tower in Ipswich, the county town. The incumbent was more than willing to accept the colours, but his archdeacon was not, and ordered that they be taken down at once. His wishes had to be obeyed, and the colours were removed to the colonel's residence elsewhere in the county.

Once a stand of colours had been replaced it became the personal property of the colonel. Some colonels kept the colours in the family, while others disposed of them straight away. When a new stand was presented to the 25th Foot at Newcastle-on-Tyne in 1763, its predecessor, by then precisely 20 years old and carried from Fontenoy to Minden and Wilhelmsthal, was buried with full military honours. In about 1856 the old colours of the same regiment were cut up and distributed as souvenirs amongst its officers. The colours of the 50th, carried during the Peninsular campaign, were 'cremated' in 1815, and the remains placed in a box bearing the names of those who fell whilst carrying them (although this story, common in the regiment at one time, may be apocryphal). A far more singular fate awaited a stand of the 19th Foot in 1827. When Lt.Col. Alexander Milne died at Demerara on 5 November that year, his dying wish was that he should be buried in the colours – and his request was granted. In the following year a Capt. Mason of the 4th Foot, about to marry the colonel's daughter, received a King's Colour as a wedding present!

The new Rifle regiments, the 60th and 95th, were not issued with colours at the time of their conversion at the beginning of the 19th century, their skirmishing tactics rendering flags an unnecessary burden

The simple centre of the Second Colour of the 86th (Leinster) Foot, from the Return of 1806. Sheet: yellow. Centre: crimson, gold lettering, within a yellow border. The King's Colour of this stand was tied to a flagstaff by a soldier of the regiment under fire to denote the successful capture of a redoubt on the island of Bourbon. Sources: Milne, *Standards and Colours*; Laurie, G.B., *History of the Royal Irish Rifles* (London, 1914).

A camp colour of the 97th Foot. Sheet: yellow. Lettering: white. Camp colours are discussed in the first part of this study, Elite 77: *British Colours & Standards 1747–1881 (1).*

Reverse of a recruiting flag used by Jane Maxwell, Duchess of Gordon, in raising men for the 2nd Battalion, Gordon Highlanders in 1803. Sheet: yellow. The Gordon family crest of a stag is prominent, as is a regimental bonnet, and a swag of the regimental tartan. The obverse depicted the Royal arms. Source: Lennox, C.H.G., *Catalogue of Weapons, Battle Trophies and Regimental Colours...* (Elgin, 1907).

without any real role on the battlefield. At the same time the light infantry regiments, which had also abandoned the linear tactics of conventional infantry, were still obliged to carry colours. Attitudes remained confused. The office of the Commander-in-Chief wrote to the regimental agent of the 90th: 'it is proper that the Light Infantry regiments should have colours, tho' when employed in active service it may be unnecessary from the description of these corps to take them into the field.' Following this advice, it appears that the 51st, 68th and 71st did not carry their colours in the Peninsula, although the 43rd and 52nd most certainly did. In addition, the 2/60th remained organised as a light infantry battalion until 1822, and was thus obliged to carry a stand of colours even though the rest of the regiment did not do so.

The light infantry and rifles were the only regiments given *official* permission to lay aside their colours. Others did so on receipt of a specific order, given either by their colonel or by the general officer commanding. At the start of the Ticonderoga campaign of 1758, Maj.Gen.Abercrombie ordered that regiments should not carry their colours, nor even their camp colours, into the field. In the forested country they faced, Abercrombie probably considered the flags a hindrance if flown and an extra burden if carried in the baggage. During the Saratoga campaign 20 years later, an officer of one of the Brunswick regiments recorded that 'our colours bother us a lot, and no British regiment brought any with them.' Nevertheless, at least one regiment, the 9th, was accompanied by its colours on this campaign, for an officer concealed them under his uniform to prevent their capture. Perhaps they were simply carried with the baggage. Colours were certainly carried in other theatres of the same war. The American authority Gherardi Davis states that six British colours were captured at the surrender at Yorktown, taken from the 43rd Foot, the 76th Highlanders and the 80th Foot. The 43rd and its successors, however, continue to deny that the colours were captured, and suggest instead that they were probably left behind in New York!

Provisional Battalions, formed in the Peninsula during 1812 by amalgamating elements from battalions severely reduced in strength by casualties, do not appear to have carried any colours. The constituent units of the 1st Provisional Battalion, the 2/31st and the 2/66th, both sent their colours back to their respective depots in Bristol and Lisbon. The 2nd Provisional Battalion, formed from the 2nd Battalions of the Queen's and the 53rd Foot, sent both stands to England. Other regiments failed to carry their colours in the field for rather different reasons. The case of the 71st at Waterloo is well known – the colours disappeared in 1814, after they had been used to decorate a banqueting hall at Carlton House.

BADGES AND DISTINCTIONS

The 1747 Regulations include a section headed 'Badges or Devices allowed to be worn by particular corps'; in 1751 this was altered to read, 'Devices and Badges of the Royal Regiments and of the six old Corps'. The 13 regiments included in the section that follows are: 1st Regiment, or Royal Scots; 2nd Regiment, or the Queen's Own Royal Regiment; 3rd Regiment, or The Buffs; 4th Regiment, or the King's Own Royal Regiment; 5th Regiment; 6th Regiment; 7th Regiment, or the Royal English Fuziliers; 8th Regiment, or the King's Regiment; 18th Regiment, or the Royal Irish; 21st Regiment, or the Royal North British Fuziliers;

23rd Regiment, or the Royal Welch Fuziliers; 27th Regiment, or the Inniskilling Regiment; 41st Regiment, or the Royal Invalids.

Each of these regiments displays a distinctive badge in the centre of its colours and in the three corners of the Second Colour without the Union canton. With the exception of those borne by the 2nd and the 27th, all the badges are associated with the royal house. Five of the 'English' Royal regiments (the 2nd, 4th, 7th, 8th and 41st) include the garter of the Order of the Garter; the two Scottish regiments (the 1st and 21st) bear the circlet of the Order of the Thistle. The single Welsh regiment bears the badges of the Prince of Wales. The single Irish regiment bears the device of a harp taken from the Royal coat of arms.

Of the remainder, the 3rd bears a green dragon, which (coloured red) is a royal badge. The 5th bears St George and the dragon, the badge of the Order of the Garter. The 6th bears an antelope; according to regimental tradition, this commemorates service in the Peninsula

The centre of the King's Colour of the 84th Foot (York and Lancaster). The regiment was granted its subsidiary title in 1809. This particular stand was made by native craftsmen in India between 1810 and 1814, which may account for its unusual style. Presumably the regiment was anxious to display its new badge immediately, rather than wait for a new stand to be sent out from England. Source: Milne, *Standards and Colours*.

The centres of two colours of the 27th (Inniskilling) Foot: (a) shows the more usual rendition of the castle, as it appears on the Second Colour of the 2nd Battalion, c.1810; (b) is that on the colour of the 1st Battalion, and represents the Watergate at Enniskillen. It was introduced in 1804 by the regiment's second lieutenant-colonel, Brig. Galbraith Lowry Cole, himself a Fermanagh man. The device was still in use in 1807, but was abolished by the colonel of the regiment, Lord Moira. Source: *Sprig of Shillelagh*, vol.26, 1945.

during the War of the Spanish Succession, although the antelope was also a badge of King Henry V. Each of these three regiments have the same corner badge of a rose and crown. The badge of the 27th commemorates the town where the regiment was raised.

The reason why these 13 regiments, but no others, should bear distinctive badges is open to some debate. The 'Royal' regiments may have been granted their badges to point up their particular status. The badges also seem to represent something in the nature of a reward for gallant conduct or a particular contribution to the success of the Hanoverian dynasty. The two most obvious examples here are those of the 27th and the 18th. The former saw service at the siege of Londonderry against the forces of James II, and in Flanders. The 18th bears a badge that includes a motto commemorating the regiment's valour at the siege of Namur. In 1746–47 the 4th was permitted to change its badge from crossed sceptres to the Royal crest of England (see Plate C3), perhaps as a reward for its service during the Jacobite rebellion of 1745–46.

From the time of the 1747 Warrant other regiments have also been granted distinctive badges, both as commemorations and as rewards. Amongst the 'commemorations' are the badges granted to the 72nd (Duke of Albany's), 85th (Duke of York's), 89th (Princess Victoria's), 91st (Princess Louise's) and 99th (Duke of Edinburgh's), all of which took the form of the cipher or coronet appropriate to the honorary colonel (all members of the royal house) named in their subsidiary title. Amongst the 'rewards' are those awarded to the 87th (for Barrosa), and numerous other regiments for service in India, Egypt and China.

BATTLE HONOURS

The practice of permitting individual battalions of a single regiment to serve independently of each other, thus making them potentially eligible for different honours, was a matter that required regulation, particularly once many of the war-raised battalions began to be disbanded after the fall of Napoleon. In February 1817, Horse Guards ordered that any badge or similar honour granted to a regiment more than one battalion strong was to be confined to the particular battalion concerned, except with the express authority of the Prince Regent. In July, the first permission under this rule was granted to the 1st Foot: orders were given that the honours gained by the 3rd Battalion, recently disbanded, should in future be borne by the 1st and 2nd Battalions. In 1833 the rule was relaxed, and every battalion within each regiment was allowed to bear the same honours.

When whole regiments were disbanded their honours went into abeyance. If and when a new regiment was raised bearing the same number, it did not automatically inherit the honours of its predecessor. For example, the 100th Regiment of Foot was disbanded in 1818, but its honours were not granted to the new 100th Foot (Prince of Wales's Canadian) until 1875, some 20 years after the new regiment had been raised.

The 96th Foot provides a further example of the complexities involved in these decisions. The 96th had originally been numbered as the 97th Regiment (Queen's Own Germans), and it was under this number that it had been granted, in 1802, the honour for Egypt. It was renumbered as 96th in 1816 and then disbanded in 1818. The 96th was re-raised in 1824, but did not receive the honours of its predecessor until 1874. A new 97th was raised at the same time but was apparently not considered for the revived honour.

On a smaller scale, particular elements of a single battalion could find themselves singled out for honours. The practice of detaching the flank companies from individual battalions could make them eligible for a battle honour to the exclusion of the centre companies. This happened, for example, to the flank companies of the 35th Foot, which participated at the battle of Maida in 1807 when the rest of the regiment did not take part. The honour was therefore granted to the flank companies only. However, since they did not carry colours of their own the matter remained moot, until it was decided to extend the honour to the rest of the regiment in 1818. Other examples include the 2/81st at Corunna (granted to the flank companies in 1812, and to the regiment as a whole in 1816), and the 2/66th at the Douro (1815 and 1823).

On occasion one battalion of a regiment might find itself the recipient of honours awarded to the other, on taking its colours into use. For example, both the 35th and the 56th Foot saw the colours of the 2nd Battalion taken into use by the 1st Battalion after the 2nd had been disbanded. On the other hand, in 1812 the 2nd Battalion of the 87th received the worn-out colours of their 1st Battalion.

As discussed in volume 1 of this study (Elite 77), the War Office, particularly during Lord Hill's period as Commander-in-Chief, was reluctant to grant further honours and badges. The government wished to maintain the value of such honours by ensuring that they did not

Table 5: Battle Honours of Infantry Regiments during the period of the Revolutionary & Napoleonic Wars

(The 1st, 2nd and 3rd Foot Guards are abbreviated here by their later titles of Grenadier, Coldstream and Scots Guards – GG, CG, SG; RB = Rifle Brigade, 95th; WIR = West Indies Regiment.)

Albuhera (awarded 1816 – 7, 23, 28, 31, 39, 57; 1817 – 34; 1818 – 29, 48; 1823 – 3, 66; 1825 – 60)

American War (refused 1820 – 89)

Amboyna (awarded by HEIC 1841 – 102)

Arroyo dos Molinos (awarded 1845 – 34; refused 1845 – 92)

Assaye (awarded 1807 – 74, 78)

Badajoz (awarded 1817 – 45, 74, 77; 1818 – 5, 48, 88, 94; 1819 – 7, 83; 1820 – 44; 1821 – 23, 27, 43, 52, 60, RB; 1823 – 4; 1824 – 40; 1825 – 30; 1831 – 38)

Banda (awarded by HEIC 1841 – 102)

Barrosa (awarded 1811 – 87; 1812 – GG, CG, SG; 1814 – 28; 1817 – 67; refused 1850 – 82)

Bladensburg (awarded 1826 – 85; 1827 – 4, 44; 1854 – 21)

Bourbon (awarded 1829 – 69, 86; refused 1826 – 12)

Busaco (awarded 1817 – 1, 45, 74, 88; 1819 – 9; 1821 – 43, 52; 1825 – 5; 1827 – 83; 1831 – 38; 1879 – 60)

Cape of Good Hope (awarded 1824 – 24; refused 1843 – 91)

Chrystler's Farm [sic] (refused 1850 – 49)

Copenhagen (awarded 1819 – 49; 1821 – RB)

Corunna (awarded 1811 – GG, 14; 1812 – 4, 14, 42, 50, 59, 81; 1821 – 43, 51, RB; 1823 – 26; 1825 – 5; 1827 – 6; 1830 – 92; 1831 – 38; 1832 – 1, 28; 1833 – 2, 36, 91; 1834 – 51; 1835 – 9, 23, 71; 1838 – 20; 1842 – 32; refused 1850 – 82)

Cuidad Rodrigo (awarded 1817 – 5, 45, 77, 74, 88; 1818 – 94; 1819 – 83; 1821 – 43, 52, RB)

Deig (awarded 1829 by HEIC – 102)

Detroit (awarded 1816 – 41)

Dominica (awarded 1808 – 46, WIR)

Douro (awarded 1813 – 3; 1818 – 48; 1815 – 66)

Egmont-op-Zee (awarded 1814 – 92 (originally granted as Bergen-op-Zoom in 1813); 1817 – 1; 1818 – 79; 1819 – 49; 1820 – 20, 25; 1821 – 1; 1830 – 63; refused 1849 – 55)

Egypt (awarded 1802 – CG, SG, 1, 2, 8, 10, 13, 18, 20, 23, 24, 25, 26, 27, 28, 30, 40, 42, 44, 50, 54, 58, 61, 80, 86, 88, 89, 90, 92, 97)

El Bodon (refused 1818 – 5, 77)

Fuentes d'Onor (awarded 1817 – 24, 42, 74, 88; 1818 – 71, 79; 1819 – 83; 1821 – 43, 45, 52, 60, RB; 1826 – 85; 1830 – 92).

Gibraltar (awarded 1784 – 12)

Great Gun (refused 1842 – 54)

Guadeloupe (awarded 1817 – 15, 90, WIR; 1819 – 63; 1867 – 70; refused 1844 – 70)

Hindoostan (awarded 1806 – 76; 1821 – 52, 71; 1825 – 17; 1835 – 36, after a refusal of India; 1837 – 72)

India (awarded 1807 – 75; 1823 – 65, 86; 1826 – 67, 69, 84; 1836, after a refusal 1832 – 12; 1838 – 14; refused 1830 – 74; 1835 – 36)

Java (awarded 1820 – 14, 59, 69, 78, 89)

Lesaca (refused 1816 – 51)

Lincelles (awarded 1811 – GG, CG, SG)

Maida (awarded 1807 – 20, 27, 47, 58, 78; 1808 – 35, flank companies only, extended to whole regiment 1818; 61)

Mandora (awarded 1813 – 92; 1817 – 90)

Marabout (awarded 1841 – 54)

Martinique (awarded 1816 – 7, 8, 13, 23; 1817 – 15, 60, 90; 1819 – 25; refused 1844 – 70)

Mauritius (refused 1826 – 12)

Miami (awarded 1816 – 41)

Monte Video (awarded 1817 – 38; 1821 – RB; 1824 – 40, 87; refused 1842 – 7)

Moro (permitted to resume 1827 – 56; refused 1829 – 15)

Niagara (awarded 1815 – 1, 8, 41, 89, 100; 1816 – 6, 82)

Nieuport (awarded 1825 – 53)

Nive (awarded 1817 – 1, 42, 57; 1818 – 59, 71, 79, 84, 91; 1819 – 9, 28, 50; 1821 – 43, 52, RB; 1823 – 3, 4, 11, 31, 34, 61, 66; 1824 – 39; 1825 – 36, 5/60; 1826 – 85; 1830 – 92; 1831 – 32, 38; 1844 – 62; 1845 – 76)

Nivelle (awarded 1816 – 11, 32, 36, 51, 61; 1817 – 1, 5, 42, 45, 57, 74; 1818 – 48, 79, 88, 91, 94; 1819 – 2, 9, 28, 83; 1820 – 53, 1821 – 23, 27, 43, 52, 58; 1821 – 5/60, RB; 1823 – 3, 31, 34, 66, 68; 1824 – 4, 24, 39, 40, 82, 87; 1827 – 6; refused 1838 – 19)

Nundy Droog (awarded 1841 – 102)

Orthes (awarded 1817 – 20, 24, 42, 45, 74, 88; 1818 – 5, 6, 48, 71, 91, 94; 1819 – 7, 28, 50, 83; 1821 – 23, 27, 52, 58, 5/60, RB; 1823 – 11, 34, 61, 66, 68; 1824 – 39, 40, 82, 87; 1826 – 32; 1830 – 92; 1834 – 51; 1836 – 36; 1847 – 31)

Peninsula (awarded 1815 – 3/1 (whole regiment 1817), 2, 3, 4, 5, 6, 7, 9, 10, 11, 20, 23, 2/24 (regiment 1825), 27, 28, 29, 36, 2/30 (regiment 1827), 2/31 (regiment 1825), 32, 2/34 (regiment 1817), 37, 38, 39, 40, 42, 43, 44, 45, 47, 48, 50, 51, 52, 2/53 (regiment 1829), 56, 57, 58, 2/59 (regiment 1816), 60, 61, 2/62 (regiment 1829), 66, 67, 68, 71, 74, 76, 77, 79, 81, 82, 83, 2/84 (regiment 1818), 85, 87, 88, 91, 92, 93, 94, RB, 97)

Pyrenees (awarded 1817 – 20, 24, 42, 45, 57, 74; 1818 – 6, 48, 71, 79, 91; 1819 – 2, 7, 28, 50; 1820 – 53; 1821 – 23, 27, 58; 1823 – 3, 11, 31, 34, 61, 66, 68; 1824 – 39, 40, 82; 1825 – 36, 60; 1826 – 32; 1830 – 92; 1834 – 51)

Queenstown (awarded 1816 – 41, 49)

Roleia (awarded 1812 – 29; 1817 – 5, 45; 1818 – 71; 1820 – 9; 1821 – 60, RB; 1824 – 40; 1825 – 82; 1826 – 32; 1827 – 6; 1831 – 38; 1832 – 36; 1833 – 91)

Salamanca (awarded 1816 – 2, 11, 32, 36, 53, 61; 1817 – 1, 5, 7, 38, 45, 74, 88; 1818 – 48, 79, 94; 1819 – 9, 83; 1820 – 44; 1821 – 23, 27, 43, 52, 58, 60, RB; 1823 – 4, 68; 1824 – 24, 40; 1825 – 30; 1834 – 51)

St Lucia (awarded 1818 – 64; 1821 – 1; 1825 – 53; 1836 – 27 after a refusal 1822; refused 1824 – 5; 1844 – 70; 1849 – 55)

St Vincent (refused 1854 – 69)

San Sebastian (awarded 1817 – 1, 38; 1818 – 47, 59; 1819 – 9; 1823 – 4)

Seringapatam (awarded 1818 – 12, 33, 73, 74, 75, 77, 94, by HEIC 1822 – 103; refused 1854 – 19)

Surinam (awarded 1818 – 64)

Talavera (awarded 1812 – CG, SG; 1816 – 48; 1817 – 24, 45, 88; 1818 – 29, 53; 1819 – 7, 9 (withdrawn 1820), 83; 1821 – 60, 61; 1823 – 3, 31, 66; 1824 – 40, 87)

Tarifa (awarded 1812 – 87; 1816 – 47)

Ternate (awarded by HEIC 1841 – 102)

Toulouse (awarded 1816 – 11, 36, 42, 61, 79, 91; 1817 – 45, 74, 88; 1818 – 5, 48, 94; 1819 – 2, 7; 1820 – 28, 53; 1821 – 23, 43, 52, 60, RB; 1824 – 40, 87; 1826 – 20; 1827 – 83)

Tournay (awarded 1825 – 53; 1826 – 37; 1836 after a refusal 1831 – 14; refused 1832 – 12; 1854 – 19)

Valenciennes (refused 1831 – 14)

Vimiera (awarded 1812 – 50; 1816 – 36; 1817 – 45; 1818 – 29, 71; 1820 – 19; 1821 – 38, 43, 52, 60, 1RB; 1824 – 40, 82; 1825 – 5; 1826 – 32; 1827 – 6; 1833 – 2, 91; 1838 – 20)

Vittoria (awarded 1816 – 28, 51; 1817 – 1, 5, 34, 74; 1818 – 47, 59, 71, 88, 94; 1819 – 2, 7, 9, 50, 83; 1820 – 53; 1821 – 23, 27, 43, 52, 58, 60, RB; 1823 – 4, 31, 66, 68; 1824 – 24, 39, 40, 82, 87; 1826 – 20; 1827 – 6; 1830 – 92; 1831 – 38)

Waterloo (awarded 1815 – 3/1 (whole regiment 1817), 4, 3/14 (regiment 1845), 23, 27, 28, 2/30 (regiment 1827), 32, 33, 40, 42, 2/44 (regiment 1816), 51, 52, 2/69 (regiment 1818), 71, 73, 79, 92, RB; refused 1843 – 91)

Abyssinia (awarded 1868 – 4, 26, 33, 45)

Aden (awarded by HEIC c.1841 – 103)

Affghanistan [sic] (awarded 1840 – 2, 13, 17; 1842 – 101)

Afghanistan 1878–79 (awarded 1881 – 17, 70, 81, RB)

Afghanistan 1878–80 (awarded 1881 – 5, 8, 12, 25, 51, 59, 60, 67, 72, 92)

Afghanistan 1879–80 (awarded 1881 – 7, 9, 11, 14, 15, 18, 63, 66, 78, 85)

Ahmed Khel (awarded 1881 – 59, 60)

Ali Musjid (awarded 1881 – 17, 51, 81, RB)

Aliwal (awarded 1847 – 31, 50, 53)

Alma (awarded 1855 – GG, CG, SG, 1, 4, 7, 19, 20, 21, 23, 28, 30, 33, 38, 41, 42, 44, 47, 49, 50, 55, 63, 68, 77, 79, 88, 93, 95, RB)

Arabia (awarded 1823 – 65)

Ashantee (awarded 1876 – 23, 42, RB, 1/WIR)

Ava (awarded 1826 – 1, 13, 38, 41, 44, 45, 47, 54, 87, 89, 102)

Balaclava (awarded 1855 – 93)

Beni Boo Ali (awarded by HEIC 1831 – 103)

Bhurtpore (awarded 1826 – 14, 59)

Bushire (awarded 1859 – 64; by HEIC 1861 – 104)

Cabool (awarded 1844 – 9, 13, 31, 40, 41)

Candahar (awarded 1843 – 41; 1844 – 40)

Canton (awarded 1861 – 59)

Cape of Good Hope (awarded 1824 – 24; 1835 – 71, 93; 1836 – 59, 72, 83)

Central India (awarded 1863 – 71, 72, 80, 83, 86, 88, 95, 108, 109)

Charasia (awarded 1881 – 67, 72, 92)

Chillianwallah (awarded 1852 – 24, 29, 61; by HEIC – 104)

China (awarded 1843 – 18, 26, 49, 55, 98)

Delhi 1857 (awarded 1863 – 8, 52, 60, 61, 75, 101, 104)

Ferozeshah (awarded by HEIC – 101; by Crown 1847 – 9, 29, 31, 50, 62, 80)

Ghuznee (for the engagement of 1839, awarded by HEIC 1839 – 102; 1840 – 2, 13, 17; for engagement of 1842, awarded 1844 – 40, 41)

Goojerat (awarded 1852 – 10, 24, 29, 32, 53, 60, 61; by HEIC 1853 – 103, 104)

Hyderabad (awarded 1844 – 22)

Inkerman (awarded 1855 – GG, CG, SG, 1, 4, 7, 19, 20, 21, 23, 28, 30, 33, 38, 41, 44, 47, 49, 50, 55, 57, 63, 68, 77, 88, 95, RB)

Jellalabad (awarded 1842 – 13)

Kabul 1879 (awarded 1881 – 9, 67, 72, 92)

Kandahar 1881 (awarded 1881 – 7, 60, 66, 72, 92)

Khelat (awarded 1840 – 2, 17)

Kirkee (awarded by HEIC 1823 – 103)

Koosh-Ab (awarded 1859 – 64, 78; by HEIC 1861 – 104)

Lucknow, Capture of (awarded 1863 – 5, 10, 20, 23, 34, 38, 42, 53, 78, 79, 84, 90, 93, 97, 101, 103, RB)

Lucknow, Defence of (awarded 1863 – 5, 32, 64, 78, 84, 90, 102)

Lucknow, Relief of (awarded 1863 – 5, 8, 23, 53, 75, 82, 84, 93)

Maharajpore (awarded 1844 – 39, 40)

Maheidpore (awarded 1823 – 1)

Mediterranean (awarded 1856 – Royal Berkshire Militia, East Kent Militia, 1st and 3rd Royal Lancashire Militia, Northamptonshire Militia, Oxfordshire Militia, King's Own Staffordshire Militia, Royal Wiltshire Militia, 2nd West York Militia, 3rd Royal Westminster Militia)

Meeanee (awarded 1844 – 22)

Moodkee (awarded 1847 – 9, 31, 50, 80)

Mooltan (awarded 1852 – 10, 32, 60; by HEIC 1853 – 103)

Nagpore (awarded 1823 – 1)

New Zealand (awarded 1870 – 58, 96, 99)

New Zealand 1860–61 (awarded 1870 – 12, 14, 40, 57, 65)

New Zealand 1863–66 (awarded 1870 – 12, 14, 18, 43, 50, 68, 70)

Pegu (awarded 1853 – 18, 51, 80; by HEIC – 101, 103)

Peiwar Kotal (awarded 1881 – 8, 72)

Pekin (awarded 1861 – 1, 2, 3, 31, 44, 60, 67, 99)

Persia (awarded 1859 – 64, 78; by HEIC 1861 – 106)

Punjaub (awarded 1852 – 10, 24, 29, 32, 53, 60, 61, 98; by HEIC 1853 – 103, 104)

Punniar (awarded 1844 – 3, 50)

Reshire (awarded 1859 – 64; by HEIC 1861 – 106)

Scinde (awarded 1843 – 22)

Sevastopol (awarded 1855 – GG, CG, SG, 1, 3, 4, 7, 9, 13, 14, 17, 18, 19, 20, 21, 23, 28, 30, 31, 33, 34, 38, 39, 41, 42, 44, 46, 47, 48, 49, 50, 55, 56, 57, 62, 63, 68, 71, 72, 77, 79, 82, 88, 89, 90, 93, 95, 97, RB)

Sobraon (awarded by HEIC 1846 – 101; by Crown 1849 – 9, 10, 29, 31, 50, 53, 62, 80)

Taku Forts (awarded 1861 – 1, 2, 3, 31, 44, 60, 67)

become too commonplace. The reasons given for refusing them to cavalry regiments were often capricious in their application, and this remains equally true for the larger number of infantry regiments that were pressing for honours after the end of the Napoleonic Wars.

In 1835 the 36th Foot applied for a distinction, such as the badge of a tiger or an elephant, to commemorate their service in India between 1790 and 1792, during the Third Mysore War against Tippoo Sahib. They were thoroughly rebuffed by Lord Hill: 'At so very remote period of time, the introduction of such distinctions on account of a remote service is found to be attended with inconvenience and objections, not the least of which is that of rendering distinctions too common throughout the Army.' Honourable distinctions, he continued, were not needed to establish the character of the regiment. 'It is hoped you will no longer feel disposed to press the subject... The 52nd, for instance, was long in India, and as actively employed... yet the former regiment has never thought it necessary, or advisable, to apply for such distinctions.'

OPPOSITE **The centre of the colour of the 1/12th Foot, whose laying-up in the church of St Mary le Tower in Ipswich in 1849 so offended the archdeacon. Sheet: yellow. Source: Monier-Williams, *The Story of the Colours*.**

The centre of the Second Colour of the 87th Foot (Prince of Wales's Own Irish), bearing the motif of the French regimental eagle captured by Sgt. Patrick Masterson of the 87th at Barrosa, 5 March 1811. Sheet: blue. Eagle, harp: gold. The Prince of Wales's plumes placed on gold rays. Source: Milne, *Standards and Colours*.

Honours, quite rightly, were restricted to regiments that had seen hard service. Writing to an unnamed regiment in 1837 (it may have been the 35th Foot), Lord Hill stated that he 'would not feel justified in recommending to His Majesty the assumption of a regimental badge or honorary distinction for any but arduous service in the field, in which the troops claiming the distinction suffered severely in action.' The application of the regiment in question, for the honour La Valette, was turned down on the grounds that it had submitted no casualty return for the action, and that there was no precedent for granting a distinction based on the successful outcome of a blockade.

The War Office set an arbitrary date for service before which it would not entertain any application. In 1831 another regiment with service in India, the 39th, attempted to have the battle of Plassey (1757) commemorated on its colours. Its application was disallowed, 'under the rules established by the late Duke of York, due to the frequency of such applications, that such distinctions were to be restricted to actions subsequent to Plassey.' The 39th persisted, however, and in November 1835 succeeded in obtaining the grant of Plassey as a battle honour, as well as the motto *Primus in Indis*, to commemorate the fact that the 39th was the first British regiment to serve on the sub-continent.

Only seven years earlier, the cut-off date had been the battle of Minden (1759). The 5th Foot was refused its application for this honour, again on the grounds that only actions subsequent to that date could be considered. Curiously, the War Office ignored the rather more compelling reason that the regiment had played no part in the battle. In 1825 the same regiment found that the date had been moved again, this time to deny its request for the honour St Lucia for the campaign of 1778.

It was obvious that no honour would be granted for a defeat; but some victories seem to have been excluded as well. The 89th Foot applied for battle honours for the War of 1812, including Chrysler's Farm (for which a clasp had been awarded to the General Service Medal) and Buffalo. Service in Canada, the regiment was informed, 'however meritorious', was not the type of action for which distinctions were usually granted. The 49th Foot, one of the regiments serving alongside the 89th in America, was equally unsuccessful. But when the same regiment, in 1834, attempted to secure

honours for Bunker's Hill *[sic]* and Brandywine, fought during the American War of Independence, the Commander-in-Chief was 'inclined to favour the request'. The 49th eventually failed in their application, however, since they were not mentioned in the dispatches of Lt.Gen. Gage, the commander at the time of the action.

In 1821 the 25th Foot sought to add the name 'Howe' to its colours and appointments, to commemorate service as marines under Admiral Lord Howe, but this was expressly forbidden: 'The C-in-C cannot recommend His Majesty to permit any regiment to assume the name of a subject as a badge of honour upon its appointments', came the reply. It was contrary to the spirit, if not the letter, of the 1747 Regulations and subsequent warrants as they were interpreted at the time.

In 1836 the 69th Foot also wished to commemorate a period of service as marines, under Lord Rodney in the West Indies in 1782. They claimed that the regiment had been awarded the distinction of a laurel wreath for the campaign, but could not produce any evidence in substantiation. If this had been forthcoming, then Lord Hill would have had no objection to it being borne on the colours. But as for wearing it on the uniform – as the regiment had also suggested – His Lordship had 'upon principle a strong objection to the restoration of obsolete badges', adding, 'in his opinion no advantage can arise to the regiment claiming… to resume a badge… it has voluntarily discontinued at some former period.' Further, he argued, it would be 'wholly inadmissible' for the regiment to 'ape' the motto of the Royal Marines.

The attempts of the colonel of the 5th (Northumberland) Foot, Gen.Sir Henry Johnson Bt, to obtain distinctions for his regiment show a degree of persistence quite beyond the norm. In 1824 the regiment was questioned on the matter of the white feather it professed to bear in commemoration of the defeat of French grenadiers on the island of St Lucia in 1778. At the same time, its claim to the honour Minden was turned down, and it was instructed to apply for the honour St Lucia through the general officer commanding at the time. The following year its request for St Lucia was rejected, and the regiment was further questioned about its use of the motto *Quo fata vocant*. By 1829 the 5th had been instructed that it could no longer bear the white feather, and was seeking permission to replace it with a red-over-white plume. A request for the honour El Bodon, an engagement that took place in the Peninsula in 1811, was then turned down on the grounds that no medal had been issued for the battle. In 1831 the regiment was at least confirmed in possession of its motto, but now had its Third Colour disallowed as well. It was certainly in an attempt to soften the effect of this final blow that the regiment was converted to fusiliers in 1836, and at last permitted to bear a battle honour, Wilhelmsthal, unique to itself (even though it was not the only regiment engaged in that action).

A lack of battle honours undoubtedly dented regimental self-esteem. Although the 16th (Bedfordshire) Foot had been raised in 1688, its colours did not carry a single battle honour until the report of the Alison Committee in 1882 at last granted the regiment honours for Marlborough's four great battles. Horse Guards attempted to allay concerns about such a state of affairs. In correspondence with the 89th Foot in 1814, it confirmed that His Royal Highness [the Prince Regent] 'would still further and more deeply regret, if ever the idea should go abroad or prevail in the army, that the gallantry of a regiment could be in any degree questionable, or its situation be considered irksome,

The blue Regimental Colour of the 85th, from the same stand as the King's Colour illustrated previously. The stand was presented in 1877 at Lucknow by the Duke of Buckingham. The regimental motto, restored to the regiment in 1839, is displayed in a large scroll below the centre. Source: Barrett, *85th King's Light Infantry.*

because the fate of war had not afforded it equal opportunities of acquiring distinctions, and obtaining those Insignia of merit, which other more fortunate, but perhaps not more deserving corps, have become entitled to.' And the 16th, along with others in the same situation, had to be content with that.

AUXILIARY FORCES

The Militia

During peacetime the Militia came under the authority of the Home Office until 1852, when control passed to the War Office. From 1855 the responsibilities of the Inspector of Regimental Colours were extended to include the regiments of the Militia, and the design of their colours fell into step with those of the Regular Army.

Some colours were presented by local towns; in 1799, for example, the Corporation of Gloucester presented a new stand to the Royal North Gloucestershire Militia. Others were supplied by the Ordnance Department, which also took charge of the alterations needed after Union with Ireland in 1801, as in the case of the colours of the Worcestershire Militia, as well as those of the Royal North Gloucesters so recently presented. In 1805 the Ordnance Department decided to allow each militia regiment a new stand of colours every 12 years or an allowance of £18 10s in lieu. By 1854 the allowance had seen scarcely any increase, and stood at £20. By 1868, however, the grant had at last been raised to £30 for a stand of two colours, although the Militia Regulations now required that the colours last at least 30 years.

1

2

3

4

1: Third Captain's Colour, 1st Foot Guards, 1747
2: Major's Colour, 3rd Foot Guards, 1770
3: 13th Company Colour, 2nd Bn.,
   Coldstream Guards, 1815
4: Royal Standard, Grenadier Guards, 1832

1

2

3

1: Lt.Hon. Robert Lindsay, 1st Bn.,
   Scots Fusilier Guards;
   The Alma, 20 Sept 1854
2: Royal Colour, Scots Fusilier Guards, 1854
3: Regimental Colour, 1st Bn.,
   Coldstream Guards, 1856

B

1: King's Colour, 11th Foot, 1751
2: Second Colour, 2nd Foot, 1751
3: Second Colour, 2nd Bn., 4th Foot, 1757
4: Second Colour, 33rd Foot, 1771

1: Lt. Mathew Latham, 3rd (E.Kent) Foot
(The Buffs); Albuhera, 11 May 1811
2: King's Colour, 3rd (E.Kent) Foot
(The Buffs), 1811
3: Second Colour, 2nd Bn.,
40th (2nd Somersetshire) Foot, 1799

D

1

2

3

4

1: King's Colour,
  90th (Perthshire Volunteers) Foot, 1802
2: Second Colour, 94th Foot (Scotch Brigade), 1812
3: Second Colour, 42nd (Royal Highland) Foot, 1809
4: Honorary Colour, 74th Foot (Highlanders), 1807

1: Second Colour, 88th Foot
    (Connaught Rangers), 1817
2: King's Colour, 3rd Bn., 1st Foot
    (Royal Scots), 1817
3: Second Colour,
    28th (N.Gloucestershire) Foot, 1821
4: Royal Colour,
    5th (Northumberland) Foot, 1839

F

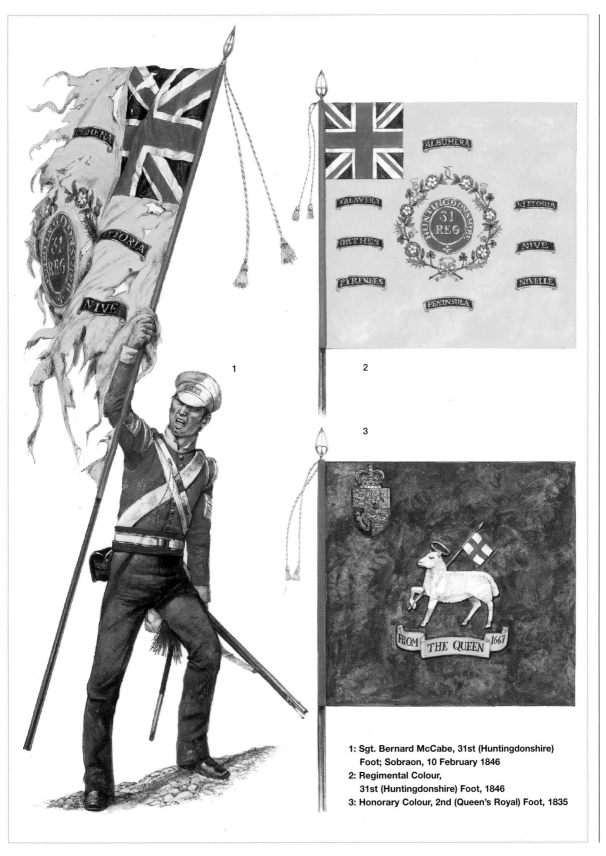

1: Sgt. Bernard McCabe, 31st (Huntingdonshire)
   Foot; Sobraon, 10 February 1846
2: Regimental Colour,
   31st (Huntingdonshire) Foot, 1846
3: Honorary Colour, 2nd (Queen's Royal) Foot, 1835

1

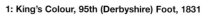

1: King's Colour, 95th (Derbyshire) Foot, 1831
2: Regimental Colour, 55th (Westmoreland) Foot, 1850
3: Regimental Colour,
   14th (Buckinghamshire) Foot, 1876
4: Regimental Colour, 1st Bn.,
   24th (2nd Warwickshire) Foot, 1879

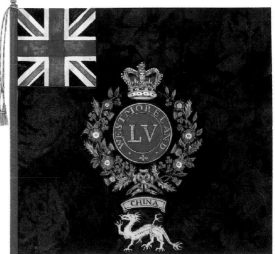

2

3

4

H

1: Ensign, Wiltshire Militia, 1760
2: County Colour, Wiltshire Militia, 1760
3: Second Colour, Agbrigg Local Militia, 1808

1: Second Colour, 1st British Fencibles
   (Glengarry Regt.), 1803
2: Second Colour, Beverley Volunteers, 1808
3: Colour, Independent Tyreril Volunteers
   & Loyal Liney Volunteers, 1778
4: Regimental Colour, Robin Hood Rifles, 1859

The Second Colour of the Temple Bar & St Paul's Association, 1794. The sheet follows the colour of the unit's blue facings. Badge: silver. Wreath: gold. Scroll: red with gold lettering and edging. Source: actual flag. (Photo National Army Museum 4174)

Since they were not subject to full time War Office control, the militia felt able to ignore the letter of the regulations concerning colours, particularly in the matter of coats of arms. Many militia regiments bore the arms of the lord lieutenant of the county, their nominal commander, on their Second Colour (known in several regiments as the 'County Colour'). Lawson, in the second volume of his *History of the Uniforms of the British Army*, gives a list of English and Welsh militia colours of the period 1759–60 gleaned from a number of documents in the Public Record Office. Of the 43 regiments listed, only five (Buckinghamshire, Cheshire, Cornwall, Hertfordshire and Pembroke) carried colours bearing a principal device that symbolised the county rather than their commander; and, of these, the devices of Buckinghamshire, Cheshire and Cornwall were all derived from personal arms or badges. The rest all bore the arms of the lord lieutenant. At a slightly later period, at least one stand belonging to the East London Militia, carried around 1780, bore the arms of the lord mayor – in this case, Sir Watkin Lewis, mayor in 1780–81.

The centre of the Second Colour of the York Chasseurs. The Chasseurs were uniformed as a rifle regiment, in green uniforms with red facings, but appear to have been classed only as light infantry – hence the colour here, white with a red cross, as for all regiments with red facings. Source: *JSAHR*, vol.14, p.235.

The Second Colour of the Royal Cornwall Militia, c.1812. Sheet: blue with gold lettering. Shield: black with fifteen gold balls. Circlet: gold with black lettering. The device of 15 gold balls on a black shield derives ultimately from the arms of Richard, Earl of Cornwall during the 13th century, but has subsequently come to symbolise the county as a whole. Source: National Army Museum microfilm 6807/28.

This style of colour was, however, losing favour in some counties at the beginning of the 19th century. Perhaps under the influence (at this stage still unofficial) of the Inspector of Regimental Colours, personal arms gradually disappeared from militia colours. In 1806, for example, the colours of the 1st Royal Lancashire Militia bore only the regimental name within a Union wreath. Where local symbols were available, they were used instead – a white rose for the 3rd West York Militia, granted in 1811, or the white horse of the West Kent Militia. These symbols were borne in the centre of the colours, within a circlet inscribed with the regimental name, exactly like the colours of the regiments of the Regular Army.

Like the 1st Royal Lancashires, some regiments of Local Militia, raised from 1808 onwards, also carried quite simple colours. The Second Colours of such stands bore the regimental name in gold letters within a Union wreath, painted directly onto the sheet. The National Army Museum holds a microfilm copy of what appears to be a pattern book, or at the very least an aide-memoire, belonging to a contemporary herald painter or flag maker. Of some 160 local militia colours depicted in its pages, the great majority follow this style; only about a quarter show any kind of device.

Some regiments still bore personal arms – for example, the Western Regiment of Royal Perthshire Local Militia, or the Agbrigg Local Militia depicted as Plate I3. Others continued to use local devices, like county symbols or municipal coats of arms. The Blackburn Hundred Higher Division Local Militia carried the red rose of Lancashire, and several

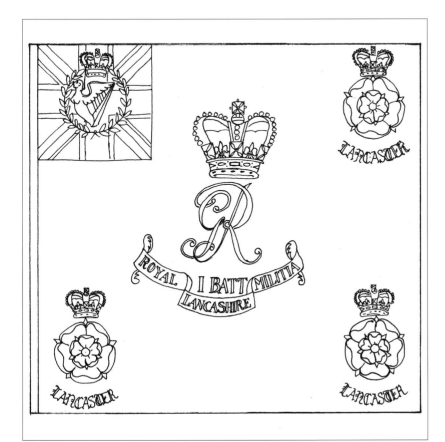

The Second Colour of the 1st Royal Lancashire Militia, 1816. Sheet: blue. Lettering and cipher: gold. Scrolls: blue with gold lettering. Corner badges: red roses with gold lettering. The colours were presented by the Lord Lieutenant of Ireland, which accounts for the most irregular gold harp in the canton. Source: Williamson, R.J.T., *History of the Old County Regiment of Lancashire Militia* (London, 1888).

45

The Second Colour of the Queen's Own Tower Hamlets Light Infantry Miitia, c.1875. Sheet: blue. Badge: silver Tower of London within red garter with gold lettering and edge. The Union wreath has been reduced to a mere spray of rose and thistle in the bottom centre of the wreath of oakleaves and acorns. Source: actual flag. (Photo National Army Museum 6678)

WESTMORLAND
EAST & WEST WARDS
LOCAL MILITIA

regiments displayed the white rose of Yorkshire. The Holland and Boston Local Militia carried the arms of Boston, Lincolnshire, on its colour. The colour of the Eastern and Central Oxfordshire Local Militia was most unusual in that the device on the obverse (the arms of Oxford) was different from that on the reverse (the arms of the University). Many local militia regiments were formed by converting regiments of Volunteers. One Lancashire unit proudly retained its old title, their colours proclaiming them to be the 'First Middleton Local Militia late Ashton-under-Lyne Volunteers'.

In 1881 the militia battalions of the new post-Cardwell regiments were allowed the badges and distinctions of their parent formation, except when awarded for actions in which they did not participate. This did not grant them a great deal. Many militia regiments, by the very nature of their service, had never been sent abroad, and with the exceptions of the invasion of Jersey in 1781, and of Wales in 1797, no battle honours had

The Second Colour of the Westmoreland East & West Wards Local Militia, c.1810. Sheet: blue. Crest: silver, standing on a gold and black heraldic torse. Garter: blue with gold lettering. Scroll: white with black lettering. Lettering: gold. The crest is that of the Lowther family, Earls of Lonsdale and lords lieutenants of the county. Source: National Army Museum microfilm 6807/28.

The centre of the buff Second Colour of the Hoddesdon & Stanstead Volunteers (Hertfordshire), c.1802. The deer is a device commonly found in this area, based upon the punning use of the word 'hart'. Source: Sainsbury, J.D., *The Hertfordshire Regiment* (Ware, 1988).

ever been awarded for engagements within the British Isles. However, the honour Mediterranean was granted after the end of the Crimean War to the ten militia regiments that had acted as guards over Russian prisoners-of-war.

The Volunteers

Like the Yeomanry discussed in Elite 77, the many regiments of Volunteers and Fencibles raised during the Revolutionary and Napoleonic Wars adopted a wide range of devices on their colours. Some bore the arms of the individual most active in raising the unit. For example, the Loyal Newborough Volunteer Association (raised in Caernarvonshire in 1799) bore the family arms of Lord Newborough, their lieutenant-colonel. Others displayed the arms of the regiment's patron. Regiments that bore the title 'Prince of Wales's', for example, invariably carried his badge of the three plumes and coronet.

Another group of regiments – like the Leeds Volunteers (West Riding of Yorkshire), the Hull and County Volunteers (East Riding of Yorkshire), or the Macclesfield Volunteers (Cheshire) – bore the coat of arms of the town where they were raised. In each case, the town corporation presented the stands of colours. Other units bore

The centre of the King's Colour of the Prince of Wales's Own Fencibles, 1794. The Second Colour was yellow. Source: *JSAHR*, vol.4, p.214.

some device symbolic of their area. The Loyal Pottery Associated Infantry, raised in the region of the Five Towns in 1798, bore an urn in the centre of the sheet to symbolise the predominant local industry, and a Stafford knot in at least one corner to symbolise the county of Staffordshire. Their colour was re-used by a successor unit, the Lane End Volunteers of 1803, simply by adding a scroll to the

The centre of the single colour of the Frampton Volunteers. The star is silver with a red centre, gold cipher, and a blue garter with gold lettering. Source: *JSAHR*, vol.7, p.219–21.

sheet bearing the new title. The new unit, however, did nothing to amend the Union Flag, which remained in its pre-1801 style; nor did it change the deep red colour of the sheet, no longer appropriate for a unit with yellow facings.

Volunteer colours frequently included a suitably patriotic motto. The colours of the Loyal Stroud Volunteers (Gloucestershire) featured the words *Si Deus est nobis quis contra nos* (If God is with us, who can be against us) – used on colours and standards since the 17th century. One of the most common was *Pro aris et focis* (For hearths and homes); the Frampton Volunteers preferred *Pro Deo, rege et carissimis* (For God,

The Second Colour of the North Fencible Highlanders, 1793. Sheet: yellow. The motto is a phonetic rendering of the Gaelic *Cluì le cruidaîl* – 'Renown [only comes] with hardship'. Source: Lennox, C.H.G., *Catalogue of Weapons, Battle Trophies and Regimental Colours...* (Elgin, 1907).

the King and our loved ones), while the 1st Bn, Manchester and Salford Volunteers went one further and boasted two mottoes – *Agnoscent Britanni suam causam* (Britons will recognise their own cause) and *Ituri in sciem majores vestros posteros cogitate* (When marching to battle, think of your forefathers and of your posterity).

Some volunteer colours were made up by professional flag makers in London. Those of the Frampton Volunteers (Devon), for example, were made by Robert Horne at a total cost of £14 14s, which included 15s for a buff leather belt and 6s for a long packing case. Others were made locally. In

The Second Colour of the Royal
Kilgraston Volunteers
(Perthshire), with an unusual
Union canton. Sheet: blue.
Source: Tullibardine, *Military
History of Perthshire.*

November 1797 one George Barton of Macclesfield was paid 15s for
'making a standard for the infantry'. The colour of the Ulverston Light
Infantry (Lancashire), however, was an even more homespun affair,
embroidered by Mrs Burton, the mother of Myles Burton, captain of the
regiment's 4th Company.

Many regiments were presented with their colours in an impressive
ceremony, often by a local dignitary. The Duchess of Northumberland
bestowed a stand on the Launceston Corps of Volunteers (Cornwall) in
June 1795. (Although ostensibly a long way from home, the duchess's
family had a parliamentary interest in the borough.) Others were
presented by the wife of the lord lieutenant of the county, or by the wife
of the colonel or other officer of the regiment. The prominent part
played by women in these presentations was by no means accidental. In
the context of the times their involvement had great resonance,
intended to provide a vivid embodiment of the cause for which each unit
was fighting.

That cause was summed up by no less a figure than the Prince of
Wales himself. Presenting the colours of the Royal Spelthorne Legion,
he emphasised that:

'... When you view those Colours they cannot fail to remind you that
you are fighting for their defence, you are fighting for your King and
Country, for your Religion, Laws, Liberties, your Wives, your Children
and your Families, for everything that is on Earth dear and valuable to
Englishmen. Receive these Colours from my hands as the most Sacred
and Precious of all Pledges! You will spill your best Blood in their
Defence and I know it will be engraved on your Hearts that you must
maintain them pure and unsullied to the last hour of your breath!'

The 'Regimental Colour' of the 9th Lancashire Rifle Volunteer Corps, 1859. Sheet: red. Arms: white with six red lions. Flags: blue with three gold wheat-sheaves and red with three gold lions and a blue heraldic label of three points. Scrolls (including that in the central device, reading 'ANNO DECIMO VICTORIAE REGINAE'): white with black lettering, and the laurel leaves in their natural colour. Source: Crompton, W. and Venn, G., *Warrington Volunteers 1798–1898* (Warrington, 1898).

The colour of the Braid Volunteers, an Irish volunteer unit. Sheet: red. Soldier: red coat with blue facings, white turnbacks and trousers. Landscape: natural colours of blue, grey, purple and green. Wreath: gold shamrocks and gold bay leaves with red berries. Flags: green over red (hoist), blue over orange (fly). Weapons, etc.: natural colours. Scrolls: white, with red (top) or blue (bottom) reverse. The reverse of the sheet depicted a gold maiden harp and gold Irish crown on a blue background in the centre, surrounded by a similar wreath and trophy of arms. Source: Hayes-McCoy, *Irish Flags*.

THE PLATES

A1: Third Captain's Colour, 1st Foot Guards, 1747

The three regiments of Foot Guards were not mentioned by name in the 1747 Regulations. They therefore felt no need to make changes to their existing practice, and continued to carry one colour per company. The Colonel's Colour of the 1st Guards was plain crimson charged with a crown, undoubtedly a survival from 17th century usage, when the Colonel's Colour was plain and the other colours progressively more heavily decorated. The remaining colours consisted of the Union Flag bearing a badge particular to each company. There were 26 such companies: one belonging to the lieutenant-colonel, one to the major, and 24 to captains. The badge was normally borne in the centre of the sheet; in addition, the colour of the Major's Company had a pile wavy in the upper hoist corner. The cords and tassels were gold and crimson mixed for the Colonel's Colour, but plain crimson for the remainder.

In 1756 the 1st Guards adopted a crimson colour with a Union canton for the companies of the lieutenant-colonel and the major; the badges, however, remained unchanged. In the same year a new issue included extra colours for the companies of the field officers (the colonel, lieutenant-colonel and major) only, suggesting that they were required for some new purpose or amended ceremonial.

Four new companies, all Light Companies, were added to the establishment in 1793. Two of them adopted the badges of the two junior companies disbanded earlier; the other two adopted badges based upon the Royal cipher. In addition, all four companies adopted a new badge of a strung bugle horn to indicate their function. The regiment's four Grenadier Companies (Nos.1 to 4) presumably adopted their own supplementary badge of a fired grenade around the same time. These badges certainly formed part of the 1814 issue of colours, but there is no earlier record of their use. All these flank companies were abolished during the Crimean War, and their additional badges omitted from colours following the 1856 issue.

In 1803 another organisational change, which affected all three regiments of Foot Guards, saw the field officers relinquish their companies. At around the same time, the former Colonel's Colour became associated with the 1st Battalion of each regiment, the Lieutenant-Colonel's Colour with the 2nd Battalion, and the Major's Colour with the 3rd Battalion. As such, each served as the 'King's Colour' of its respective battalion, while a Company Colour, borne in rotation, served as the 'Regimental Colour'. Source: Dawnay, N.P., *The Standards, Guidons and Colours of the Household Division* (Tunbridge Wells, 1965).

A2: Major's Colour, 3rd Foot Guards, 1770

The junior regiment contained 18 companies in 1746. The colours of the three field officers had a crimson sheet, while the 15 Captains' Colours used the Union Flag. The Colonel's Colour had mixed gold and crimson cords and tassels, while the remainder had plain crimson.

Although the company badges of the two senior regiments all belonged to the Royal house, those of the Scots regiment had no connection with the Hanoverian dynasty. All are quasi-heraldic in nature, six of them including an ornamented cartouche, and are accompanied by a motto. The Lieutenant-

Colonel's Colour, Grenadier Guards, c.1828. Sheet: crimson. Lettering: gold. Grenade: black and grey with yellow and red flames. Source: Dawnay, *Standards of the Household Division*.

Colonel's Company bore a Union badge of rose and thistle combined on the same stalk, but it was originally painted in the Scottish fashion, with the thistle in the more 'honourable' position towards the hoist. Badges of this quasi-heraldic type are shown in the record of colours captured at Dunbar in 1650, and were a feature of Scottish colours during the Civil War. It is possible that the company badges of the 3rd Guards represent the devices of the captains serving in 1707, when the regiment was taken onto the British establishment. Source: Dawnay, *Standards of the Household Division*.

A3: 13th Company Colour, 2nd Battalion, Coldstream Guards, 1815

In 1746 the 2nd Guards contained the three field officers' companies and 15 Captains' Companies. Unlike the senior regiment at this time, the field officers' companies had a crimson sheet, whilst the captains used the Union Flag. The cords and tassels were identical to those used by the 1st Guards.

The Grenadier Companies of the Coldstream Guards were Nos. 1 and 2, and the Light Infantry Companies were Nos.15 and 16. All these flank companies appear to have borne the additional badges of the grenade and strung bugle horn. These appeared on their colours from 1814 until 1856, when they were removed following the general disbandment of flank companies. See also caption on page 9. Source: Dawnay, *Standards of the Household Division*.

A4: Royal Standard, Grenadier Guards, 1832

The senior company of the 1st Guards was known as the King's (or Queen's) Company and took precedence over the Colonel's Company. From the late 17th century the King's Company had its own distinctive colour. The central device was the Royal cipher while the corner devices represented the various kingdoms of the United Kingdom. In the early 18th century these were shields of arms, but by 1756 they had given way to badges similar to those shown here, with a gold fleur-de-lis representing France instead of a second English rose. The fleur-de-lis was replaced by a rose in 1801, when Britain finally relinquished its claim to the French throne.

This particular flag cost £42 to embroider. A further £2 was paid for a staff, with a 'brass gilt shoe' and an 'ornamental gilt blade' finial, a total of 10ft 8ins. in length. On 18 June 1832, King William IV decided to replace the spearhead finial with a new pattern in silver-gilt, depicting the lion and crown of the Royal crest standing on a base consisting of the Royal arms and cipher with a laurel wreath. No price is given for the replacement; a new set of cords and tassels cost a further £8.

When, in 1857, the War Office took over responsibility for supplying colours to the Army, it argued successfully that this standard was a personal gift from the sovereign, and that the cost of a replacement should not be borne by the public purse. Only one standard is now presented at the beginning of each reign. Source: Dawnay, *Standards of the Household Division*.

B1: Lieutenant Hon. Robert Lindsay, 1st Battalion, Scots Fusilier Guards; The Alma, 20 September 1854

At the battle of the Alma the Scots Fusilier Guards formed part of the Guards Brigade of the 1st Division, commanded by the Duke of Cambridge. The Scots were ordered forward to support the flank of Codrington's Light Division, which was heavily engaged in attacking the Great Redoubt. A Russian counter-attack pushed the Light Division back, taking the left wing of the regiment with them. The right wing pressed ahead, but lost much of its shape, forming a loose wedge or triangle, with the colours at the point. Although the regiment advanced to within 30 yards of the Redoubt it was counter-attacked in its turn and forced to withdraw. Given a little time to reform, the regiment went forward once more, supporting other regiments of the brigade in their successful advance.

Carrying the Colonel's Colour, Lt. Lindsay became a rallying point for part of the regiment. Some weeks later, at the battle of Inkerman, he was again prominent in rallying his men, and in leading a counter-attack. For these actions he was awarded the Victoria Cross. This figure is based on the painting by the Chevalier Desanges. The rolled-up blanket and the canvas haversack are the only items that distinguish the campaign order of this uniform from that worn on parade in Hyde Park. Source: Creagh, O'M., & Humphris, E.M., *The Victoria Cross 1856–1920* (repr. Polstead, 1983).

B2: Royal Colour, Scots Fusilier Guards, 1854

The 'Alma Colours' of the Scots Guards hang in the Church of Scotland Chapel at the Guards Depot. The stand consists of the Colonel's Colour and the Regimental Colour bearing the badge of No.1 Company (see line illustration, page 14, item *d*). The flags were presented in 1853 and carried for the usual term of seven years. Source: Dawnay, *Standards of the Household Division*.

B3: Regimental Colour, 1st Battalion, Coldstream Guards, 1856

Apart from the addition of battle honours, no other alterations were made to the regiment's colours from 1746 until 1856, when they were reduced in size.

The badge of No.15 Company was the crown of Charlemagne, a charge from the Hanoverian arms deriving from the Elector's position as Arch-Chancellor of the Holy Roman Empire. The 15th was formerly a Light Company, but with this issue the bugle horn badge was omitted. Source: Dawnay, *Standards of the Household Division*.

C1: King's Colour, 11th Foot, 1751

This flag represents the pattern of King's Colour adopted by regiments which lacked a distinctive badge. The cross of St George was specified as 13ins. wide, the white fimbration of the cross as 5ins., and the saltire as 9 inches. The Union canton on the Second Colour was 20ins. on the staff by 22ins. long.

The 11th Foot received its first stand of colours under the new regulations in 1748; these were replaced in 1762. The latter were not replaced until 1780, but this new stand was described as 'considerably worn' after only nine years of home service. Source: *JSAHR*, vol.7, p.7.

C2: Second Colour, 2nd Foot, 1751

The lamb is the most enigmatic of all British Army badges. Only regimental tradition attributes it to Catherine of Braganza, the queen of Charles II, who was on the throne when the regiment was raised. The lamb is not associated with the house of Braganza; nothing else connects Catherine with the badge, and although she is depicted with a lamb in a surviving portrait, this may be no more than a conventional device to indicate purity or gentleness. Moreover, nothing resembling a lamb appears on any of the regiment's colours at that period. The matter is complicated by the regiment's nickname, 'Kirke's Lambs', attributed in the late 17th century, when Percy Kirke was colonel; however, 'lamb' in this context may be used ironically – the former Tangier Regiment was not renowned for gentleness. The symbol is not otherwise derived from Kirke's arms. The first recorded use of the badge by the 2nd was apparently on the grenadier caps c.1720. These are illustrated on a recruiting placard where the lamb appears with the Prince of Wales's feathers, since the regiment was then called the Princess of Wales's – but the lamb is no more associated with the house of Hanover than the house of Braganza. It was not until around 1820 that the device became – again for reasons unknown – a 'paschal lamb', the Lamb of God, with a gold nimbus around its head and carrying over its shoulder a flag in white with a red cross.

The origins of the CARA cipher are also unclear. It could stand for the first and last letters of each word in CatherinA ReginA (Charles II's queen), or in CarolinA ReginA (George II's queen). Although Queen Caroline had died in 1737, before the 1747 Warrant came into force, she had been queen when the regiment received its title and is the more likely contender. The regiment later adopted a simple C, doubled and reversed; this is the cipher of Charlotte, queen of King George III. The colours may have been intended to bear the cipher of whichever queen was on the throne, but the long reign of George III ensured that the use of Queen Charlotte's cipher became a tradition.

According to Cannon's history, the regimental motto was awarded to commemorate the conduct of the 2nd at Tongres in 1703; however, this is unlikely. The motto was shared by a cavalry regiment, the 8th Hussars, which served with the 2nd on only one occasion – the battle of Almanza (1707), during a campaign in the Peninsula; perhaps, then, it was granted for this action? Yet the motto was not included in the Warrant itself; it appears only in Napier's paintings, and may not therefore have been officially authorised. It was used on the officers' appointments from c.1799, but was not officially granted (or re-granted) until 1834. Sources: Milne, S.M., *Standards and Colours of the British Army* (Leeds, 1895); *Bulletin of the Military Historical Society* (cited hereafter as *Bull. MHS*) vol.3, pp.12–14; *JSAHR*, vol.63, p.246.

C3: Second Colour, 2nd Battalion, 4th Foot, 1757

A richly embroidered colour for a short-lived battalion. The 2nd Bn, 4th Foot was formed in 1756, but two years later, in April 1758, it became a regiment in its own right as the 62nd Foot. These colours must date from the period before 1758, when the facings changed to buff. The colours eventually became the property of the colonel of the regiment, Alexander Duroure. One curious note is supplied by an Inspection Return of the 62nd, dated 1769. This states clearly that the colours then carried were presented in 1757, or when the regiment was still the 2/4th. It would have been absolutely incorrect for the 62nd to continue carrying its old, blue colours after 1758. One regimental history offers a solution, suggesting that the confusion arose from a mistake made on the part of the inspecting officer, who had simply jumped to an incorrect conclusion.

Napier's drawings for the 4th Foot show the corner badge as a crowned standing lion. Duroure has embellished the basic device with an elaborate cartouche around each badge, as well as around the regimental number in the upper hoist corner. Both bear the pile wavy designating a second battalion; on the King's Colour it extends from the corner of the sheet to the angle of the cross of St George.

The badge is taken from the English Royal crest. The regiment was given the additional title of 'King's Own' in 1715, soon after the accession of King George I. However, the colours carried by the regiment during the 1745 Jacobite Rebellion survive. They do not bear this badge, but instead one consisting of two crossed sceptres below a crown. It is possible that the badge seen here was granted as a result of the regiment's gallantry at Culloden, where it took most of the weight of the Jacobite charge. Sources: *JSAHR*, vol.8, p.32; Kenrick, N.C.E., *The Story of the Wiltshire Regiment* (Aldershot, 1963).

C4: Second Colour, 33rd Foot, 1771

A typical stand of a regiment with red facings, with the rambling wreath characteristic of the 1770s. This stand of colours was deposited in the church of St Mary Magdalene, Taunton, in 1782, when the regiment returned from America. A new set was presented in the following year. Source: Bruce, C.D., *History of the Duke of Wellington's Regiment* (London, 1927).

D1: Lieutenant Matthew Latham, 3rd (East Kent) Foot (The Buffs); Albuhera, 11 May 1811

At the battle of Albuhera the Buffs formed part of a counter-attacking force, and were caught in the open in line formation by French cavalry making a flanking attack. Blinded by a sudden storm of hail and rain, the regiment became disorganised and the enemy cavalry penetrated its ranks. The Second Colour was captured, and its bearer, the 16-year-old Ensign Thomas, was killed; Ensign Walsh, carrying the King's Colour, was wounded and sank to the ground. Lieutenant Latham immediately seized the colour and held it aloft. He was quickly set upon by a number of French and Polish cavalrymen intent on capturing the colour. A French hussar made a cut at Latham that sliced off part of his nose and opened his cheek; another cut almost severed his right arm (not his left, as is so often depicted). Still Latham clung on to the colour. Beset on all sides, he managed to tear the flag from its staff and conceal it under his tunic before collapsing. The French were driven off in their turn, and a sergeant of the 7th Fusiliers recovered the colour lying beneath Latham's body. However, the lieutenant was not dead, and survived to rejoin his regiment in 1813. He was presented with a gold medal for his bravery, and the Prince Regent himself met the expenses of his surgery. After the war Latham married a French girl and settled in France.

D2: King's Colour, 3rd (East Kent) Foot (The Buffs), 1811

The colours of the Buffs at this time are known from the return submitted by the colonel to the Inspector of Regimental Colours in 1806. The colours were presented not long after the Union with Ireland, but by 1813, according to an inspecting officer, they were 'so worn and disfigured that [he] could not report on them'. Nevertheless, they continued to be carried for another year.

The centre of the Second Colour bears the badge of a green dragon, with the regimental motto *Veteri frondescit honores* on a three-part scroll below. The dragon was a badge of Henry VII, but his was the red Welsh version. Why the colour of the beast should have been changed here remains uncertain. Source: Milne, *Standards and Colours*.

The Second Colour of the 18th Foot, 1818. The Royal Irish was one of the regiments which did not manage to acquire any battle honours during the Revolutionary and Napoleonic Wars against France. Sheet: blue. Harp: gold. Corner badges: gold on blue. Scroll: black lettering on white. Source: actual flag. (Photo National Army Museum 31741)

D3: Second Colour, Second Battalion, 40th (2nd Somersetshire) Foot, 1799

The practice of using the pile wavy to indicate the colours of a second battalion fell out of favour as the 18th century progressed. This colour, along with one belonging to the 2/20th Foot illustrated in Milne, must have been among the last to include it. The colour presented to the 2/90th in 1795 bore the figure '2' instead (see Plate E1). The Prince Regent's instruction to the 1st Foot (see Plate F2), replacing the pile with a scroll bearing the battalion number, may have been instrumental in sealing the fate of this ancient device. Source: Mullaly, B.R., *The South Lancashire Regiment (Prince of Wales's Volunteers)* (Bristol, 1955).

E1: King's Colour, 90th (Perthshire Volunteers) Foot, 1802

The regiment was raised by Thomas Graham of Balgowan in 1794; a second battalion existed between 1794 and 1796, and again between 1804 and 1817. The colours of the 1st Bn were presented by Col. Graham on 4 June 1795 and were carried until 1817.

The badge of the Sphinx was authorised on 6 July 1802. The 90th was unusual amongst line regiments in that it placed four examples of the badge on the sheet. Three further honours were granted in 1817 – Mandora, Martinique and Guadeloupe – but the colours were in too poor a

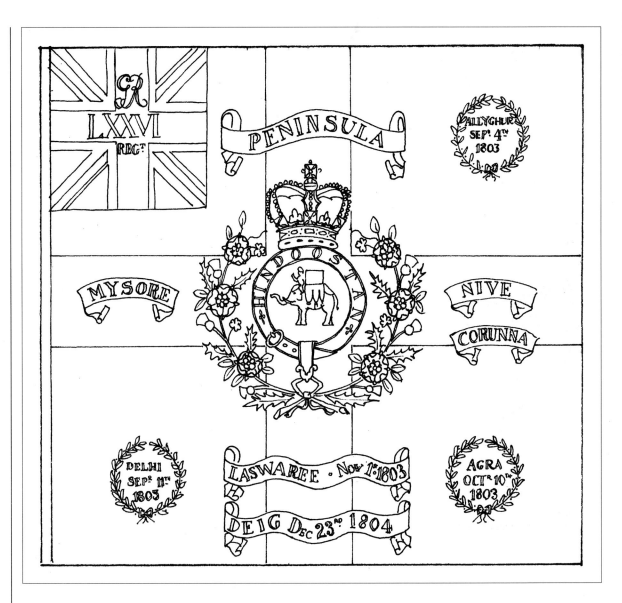

The honorary Second Colour of the 76th Foot, presented by the Honourable East India Company; see commentary to Plate E4. Sheet: white with a red cross. Scrolls and medallions: dark blue with gold lettering. The medallions read 'ALLYGUR/ SEP^R 4TH/ 1803' (top right); 'DELHI/ SEP^R 11TH/ 1803' (bottom left); and 'AGRA/ OCT^R 10TH/ 1803' (bottom right). Source: Bruce, *Duke of Wellington's Regiment*.

condition to receive them. A new stand was presented, and the honours were borne on this.

The colours of the 2nd Bn did not bear the honour for Egypt, since the battalion never left Britain. The centre of the original Second Colour bears a simple heart-shaped shield with the regimental number – REG^T XC; below the shield is a small crimson disc with the figure '2' in gold. Source: *Despatch: Journal of the Scottish Military Historical Society*, 133, pp.19–21.

E2: Second Colour, 94th Foot (Scotch Brigade), 1812

The 94th Foot was formed by the transfer of Scottish regiments from Dutch to British service in 1793. Its first stand of colours was presented at a ceremony in George Square, Edinburgh, in the same year. The original stand bore in the centre a badge of the star of the Order of the Thistle. It was retired in 1801 while the regiment was in India, and was sent home to the regiment's first colonel, Col. Ilay Ferrier. Although a replacement stand was made up in 1801, the regiment does not appear to have taken the colours into use until 1809. Three years' hard campaigning in Spain and Portugal wore them out, and they were replaced in their turn at Lisbon in 1812. The colour shown here is one of the 1812 stand.

The regiment had been granted the badge of an elephant for its service in India, particularly at Seringapatam, and this was made the centrepiece of the colour. Although the number of Scots serving in the regiment is open to question, an attempt

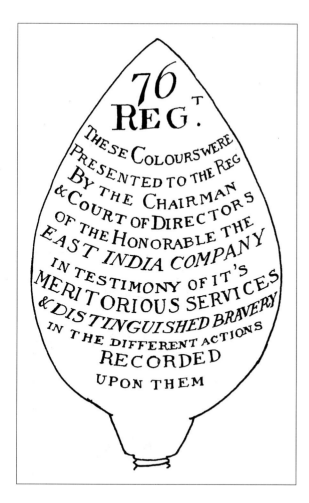

The special engraved brass finial of the honorary colour of the 76th Foot. Source: Bruce, *Duke of Wellington's Regiment.*

E3: Second Colour, 42nd (Royal Highland) Foot, 1809

The 42nd – the Black Watch – was probably granted its distinctive badges after it had been granted the subsidiary title, 'Royal Highland', in 1758. Although the use of Royal badges was common in England it was less so in Scotland. The thistle and the unicorn were both introduced as national emblems by King James III during the 15th century, but the array of badges used by the English kings was never evident north of the border. Many Scottish regiments used, or were granted, badges which contained elements from the regalia of the Order of the Thistle (originally founded by James III but refounded in 1687). These included the 1st, 21st, 42nd, 73rd, 84th Royal Highland Emigrants, 2/92nd, 94th Scotch Brigade and 100th Regiments of Foot, as well as a number of militia and volunteer units. Source: Milne, *Standards and Colours.*

E4: Honorary Colour, 74th Foot (Highlanders), 1807

Regiments, both Crown and Company, which had distinguished themselves in India were presented with an extra, honorary colour by the Honourable East India Company. This distinction was conferred on two regiments, the 74th and the 78th Foot, which had both fought at Assaye on 23 September 1803. Each colour was to bear 'a device properly suited to commemorate that signal and splendid victory.' The device chosen was an elephant surrounded by a laurel wreath and placed on a sheet in the colour of the regimental facings.

The honorary colour of the 74th appears to have been carried on parades and was certainly noted on inspection reports. Not every inspecting officer approved: 'It is a very honourable, but useless appendage, and takes one officer to carry it, who would be much better with his company', wrote Sir George Bingham. Its use in the field was discontinued by order of the Commander-in-Chief in August 1830; henceforth it was only to be carried at reviews and inspections and on gala days. It was accidentally burnt in April 1918.

The fate of the colour awarded to the 78th is unknown. It did not accompany the regiment when it spent time in Europe on occupation duties in 1817, nor is it mentioned in the regiment's inspection reports. Perhaps the colonel felt that the HEIC's award was only valid in India itself, and that the 78th was not entitled to carry a third colour after leaving the sub-continent. From the regiment's point of view, the honour was hard won, since two sergeants had been forced to carry the colours at Argaum and at Assaye after all the officers had become casualties. A regimental history notes that a colour staff found in the Arsenal at Bombay in 1879 was reputedly that of the missing colour, deposited there before the regiment left India for Java in 1811. The 78th wore buff facings, but that aside it is likely that in appearance the colour was similar to that of the 74th. In 1863 the 78th tried to obtain a replacement for the missing colour through official channels. However, its application was refused on the grounds that it was never the intention that these colours should be replaced. A second application in 1887 met with a similar response, although the regiment was told that there would be no objection should it decide to have its own colour made up, provided the flag was placed in the officers' mess and did not appear on parade. The regiment did just that in 1889.

has been made to emphasise a Scottish connection. The figures on either side of the centre, the motto, and the crest are all taken from the coat of arms of the city of Edinburgh. The motto is a version of Psalms 127:1, 'Except the Lord keep the city, the watchman waketh but in vain.' It was later re-used by the 25th Foot, another regiment with Edinburgh connections. The colours were retired in 1819, when the regiment was disbanded; they were presented to the regimental colonel, Col. James Campbell. Unusually, the regiment added to its colours none of the battle honours to which it was entitled, presumably because they were granted only weeks before it ceased to exist. The honours in question were Peninsula, Cuidad Rodrigo, Badajoz, Salamanca, Vittoria, Nive, Orthes and Seringapatam.

The 94th Foot was re-raised in 1825. When presented with its first stand of colours, reference was made to the new regiment's predecessor, but it was not permitted to display the honours from India and the Peninsula until 18 March 1874. Sources: Ross, A., *Old Scottish Regimental Colours* (Edinburgh, 1885); Jourdain, H.F.N. & Fraser, E., *The Connaught Rangers* (London, 1924).

The 76th Foot also received a pair of honorary colours from the HEIC, 'in testimony of its meritorious services and distinguished bravery in the different actions recorded upon them'. They were intended to be carried by the regiment whilst it remained in India, or until the King's pleasure be signified. The colours took the form of an ordinary stand, but with additional panels in dark blue silk edged with a gold laurel wreath, on each of which was embroidered a battle honour, also in gold. The colours were presented in Jersey on 26 January 1807, and were carried throughout the Peninsular campaign. The panels were sewn onto new cloth in 1833, and the whole was replaced with a stand donated by the India Office in 1880. The finial was a solid brass spearhead, with an engraved dedication testifying to the regiment's distinguished conduct (see line illustrations). Sources: Ross, *Old Scottish Regimental Colours*; Bruce, *Duke of Wellington's Regiment*; MacVeigh, J., *The Historical Records of the 78th Highlanders, or Ross-shire Buffs* (Dumfries, 1886).

F1: Second Colour, 88th Foot (Connaught Rangers), 1817

These colours formed the second stand bestowed upon the regiment. The first had been presented late in 1793 or early in 1794, but was replaced after the Buenos Aires campaign in 1808. According to Cannon's history, the regiment displayed on its colours a badge of a crown and harp with the motto 'Quis seperabit?'; however, there is no evidence of this on the 1808 stand. In 1830 the regiment requested permission to *retain* the use of the crown and harp, but no evidence of the original grant could be found. The badge was thus awarded to the regiment 'for the first time' on 29 January 1831.

In the 1808 stand shown here, the battle honours awarded during the Peninsular campaign were not embroidered onto separate scrolls, but attached to two long scrolls which wound their way down the width of the sheet. The colours themselves were rather the worse for wear even then, having been pierced by several balls during a number of different actions. The staffs of both colours had been hit by musket balls at Salamanca, but were later repaired and brought back into service. When this stand was retired in 1820 the sheets were removed from the staffs, which were then re-used for the new stand. This occurred again in 1834. Sources: Hayes-McCoy, G., *History of Irish Flags* (Dublin, 1979); Jourdain & Fraser, *Connaught Rangers*.

F2: King's Colour, 3rd Battalion, 1st Foot (Royal Scots), 1817

Although the 1st Foot was named the 'Royal Scots' in 1747, by 1751 its subsidiary title had been altered to 'The Royal Regiment'. Despite some opposition from within the regiment itself, the Prince Regent insisted that it resume the Scottish version of its title, and ordered a number of alterations to be made to its colours. In 1812 the centre badge was changed, and the circlet of St Andrew became the collar of the Order of St Andrew. The circlet was instead included in the corner badges, although it cannot be seen on the example shown here. The four battalions could henceforth be distinguished by the battalion number borne on a small 'label' at the junction of the two parts of the wreath, and the 2nd Bn was to abandon the pile wavy. As an extra mark of favour the 1st, 3rd and 4th Bns were permitted to bear the Sphinx and Egypt on their colours, even though only the 2nd Bn had served there. Although new stands were subject to regulation by the Inspector of Colours after 1806, the exuberant display shown here suggests that there was little he could do about additions to existing sheets.

In 1817 the 3rd Bn was disbanded and its men were drafted into the two remaining battalions. Their colours were granted the privilege of bearing the honours previously granted to the 3rd. In 1821 the regiment was permitted to resume the title of 'The Royal Regiment'. Source: Ross, *Old Scottish Regimental Colours*.

F3: Second Colour, 28th (North Gloucestershire) Foot, 1821

In common with the other regiments that took part in the Egyptian campaign, the 28th Foot was granted the badge of the Sphinx in 1802. In this stand of colours, however, that badge has been enlarged to occupy a pre-eminent central position, with the other battle honours relegated to small scrolls underneath. The regiment was justly proud of its gallant conduct at Alexandria in 1801, and no doubt wished to commemorate that action more prominently than the others. The regiment's distinctive 'back badge', commemorating the same battle, was not granted officially until 1830, although it had been worn for some years previously.

This stand, presented by the colonel of the regiment, Lt.Gen. the Hon. Sir Edward Paget, replaced the colours carried at Waterloo, which were so reduced to rags that the Sphinx badge tore away from the tattered remains of the fabric and fell to the ground. Source: Milne, *Standards and Colours*.

F4: Royal Colour, 5th (Northumberland) Foot, 1839

In addition to this and the Second Colour, of conventional design, the 5th was one of the regiments which were awarded third or 'honorary' colours. As described under Plate E4 above, two regiments received these for their service in India; the origins of two others, carried by the 2nd and 5th Foot, are uncertain.

The honorary colour carried by the 5th was described as green silk with a fringe on the three free sides, the badge of St George and the dragon in the centre, and the motto *Quo fata vocant*. A rose and crown lay in each corner, and the finial was not the customary spearhead but a crescent and laurel wreath. The flag was said to represent a French colour captured by the regiment at Wilhelmsthal in 1762, possibly belonging to the Régiment d'Aquitaine. This seems unlikely: the Régiment d'Aquitaine had no green in its colours, while green *is* the colour of the regimental facings of the 5th. Known now as the 'Drummer's Colour', it was never treated on the same basis as the colours proper. It was carried instead by a sergeant at the head of the regiment, in the rear rank of the corps of band and drums in column of route, and in the rear of the centre when in line.

At an inspection in 1805 the Duke of York had expressed his approval not only of this third colour, but of all such 'distinguishing marks or banners'. It was accidentally burnt, along with the rest of the regiment's colours, in a fire at Gibraltar in 1831, but when the regiment petitioned for all three flags to be replaced permission was obtained only for the regulation two. King William IV forbade the 5th, or any other regiment, from carrying a third colour under any circumstances. These strictures were modified slightly to allow the regiment to acquire a replacement at its own

The Second Colour of the 88th Foot (Connaught Rangers) from the stand presented in 1834, after the badge of the harp was sanctioned; cf Plate F1. Sheet: yellow. Source: Jourdain & France, *Connaught Rangers*.

expense for display in the officers' mess, with the proviso that it should never be carried on parade. Source: Milne, *Standards and Colours*.

G1: Sergeant Bernard McCabe, 31st (Huntingdonshire) Foot; Sobraon, 10 February 1846

During the Sikh War the enemy had withdrawn across the River Sutlej, leaving only one bridgehead near the village of Sobraon. There they took up an entrenched position, which the British had to assault to drive them out. The 31st Foot, together with the 47th Bengal Native Infantry and the Nussarree Battalion of Gurkhas, formed part of a brigade under Brig. Penny. This was supported by another brigade consisting of the 50th Foot and 42nd Bengal Native Infantry, under Brig. Hicks. Both were on the British right, under the overall command of Sir Harry Smith.

Both brigades had a difficult time attacking the Sikh positions – the ground was criss-crossed by dry watercourses, and the enemy fire was very heavy indeed. Both

the officers carrying the regiment's colours had been killed, and the attack had stalled, when Sgt. McCabe picked up the Regimental Colour and ran forward under fire to plant it on one of the highest parts of the Sikh entrenchments. The regiment followed, accompanied by the 50th Foot and the Gurkhas, and the position was carried. For his gallantry Sgt. McCabe was given an ensigncy in the 18th Royal Irish, and later became a captain in the 32nd. He served at the Lucknow Residency during the Indian Mutiny, where he was killed on 1 October 1857, while leading the garrison's fourth sortie against the besieging forces.

A form of campaign dress quickly evolved during the Sikh Wars, consisting of the shell jacket and locally made light trousers, worn with HEIC pattern belts. Some regiments

The obverse of the Second Colour of the Western Regiment of Royal Perthshire Local Militia, c.1810. Sheet: blue. The arms are those of the county of Perthshire: yellow shield with a red lion standing on a green mound and holding a blue sword, all within a red double border; the canton is blue with a white building and gold crown. The eagle is in its natural colours; the horse is white with a red harness. The Highlander is dressed as a soldier of the 42nd Foot. Source: Tullibardine, *Military History of Perthshire*.

retained the full-dress shako with white covers, but contemporary prints of the battle show both the 31st and the 50th wearing white or white-covered broad-crowned forage caps. McCabe served with the Light Company, and the shoulder 'wings' of his jacket bear bugle horn badges. Sources: Pearse, H.W., *History of the 31st and 70th Foot* (London, 1916), vol.1; Barthorp, M.J., *Queen Victoria's Commanders*, Elite 71 (Oxford, 2000).

G2: Regimental Colour, 31st (Huntingdonshire) Foot, 1846

As indicated in the previous plate, the Regimental Colour of the 31st was badly worn and tattered; this plate shows how it should have looked when complete. The colours were already 21 years old at Sobraon, having been presented on 7 March 1827 by Lady Amherst, the wife of the governor-general, while the regiment was stationed at Meerut. They had already been carried in action during the First Afghan War, and earlier in the Sikh War, where the regiment lost a total of nine officers and 203 men killed. The stand was carried until May 1848, when its replacement was presented to the regiment by the Duke of Cambridge.

It was not the first time that this regiment's colours had been used to spur on an attack. In December 1812, at the battle of the Nive during the Peninsular War, Gen. Byng seized the King's Colour and led a charge in person. (Byng later included the colours in his own coat of arms.)

The battle of Sobraon continued to be commemorated within the regiment (later 1st Bn, East Surrey Regiment). A fragment of the colours was placed in a salt cellar, from which every newly joined officer was invited to 'take salt with the Regiment' and to sign the Salt Book. On Sobraon Day itself the modern-day colours were delivered to the care of a sergeant and trooped through the ranks of the regiment before being installed in the Sergeants' Mess for the remainder of the day. Source: *Illustrated London News,* 19 December 1846; Pearse, *History of the 31st and 70th Foot,* vol.1.

G3: Honorary Colour, 2nd (Queen's Royal) Foot, 1835

This plate shows a reconstruction of the Honorary Colour of the 2nd Foot drawn from written descriptions. Like the 5th, the 2nd also claimed the right to carry an honorary third colour; and like the 5th, it also fell foul of William IV's refusal to allow this. The king expressed to Lord Hill his 'earnest hopes that the Queen's Royals would regard this decision not as a mark of His Majesty's forgetfulness of the uniformly high character of the regiment, but solely as a proof of His Majesty's determination to establish uniformity in this, as in every other respect, throughout the army.'

Like so much that is associated with the flags carried by this regiment, the origins of the colour shown here are obscure. They may well lie in the older practice of each company within a regiment carrying its own colours, since its original third colour was probably just an old company colour made redundant by the 1747 Regulations. It is perhaps significant that the regiment was abroad, in Gibraltar, when the 1747 Warrant was issued, and did not return to England until 1749. Against regulation, it was still parading its third colour (sea green with the arms of the colonel, one Thomas Fowkes – but no lamb...) as late as 1750, before the flag finally went into store at Kilmainham.

In 1825 it was retrieved from its resting-place, when it was found to be much tattered. A copy was made and, with the permission of King George IV, it was carried with the regiment on parade; this is the colour shown here. If the descriptions of the two colours are correct, then it is difficult to see how this flag could be a true copy of the one laid up in 1750, since it did not bear Fowkes's arms. This colour was carried until 1835, and was finally laid up in a church in Gosport in 1847.

King William's ruling countermanded that of his brother, George IV, who had first allowed the Queen's to carry this third colour in 1825. (Nor was his desire for uniformity as strong as he claimed, for he was prepared to break his own rules when presenting an extra guidon to the Royal Horse Guards in 1832 – see volume 1, Elite 77).

A second replacement was made up in 1853 at the request of the regiment. This incorporated the centre of the original colour and, for some curious reason, a crowned harp (which had never been a badge of the regiment). This colour went missing in its turn, and was replaced in 1888 by a flag different again in design. The new flag resembled the Colonel's Colour in use in 1687, with a central device of interlaced Cs on a green sheet. The regiment appears to have adhered to this pattern ever since. Source: *Bull. MHS,* vol.3, pp.12–14.

H1: King's Colour, 95th (Derbyshire) Foot, 1831

The 95th's first stand of colours had been presented in 1823 when the regiment was raised, but only three years later they were almost unserviceable because of the harmful effect of the paint on the silk of the sheet. Dissatisfied, the colonel of the regiment, Sir Archibald Campbell, decided to have the colours replaced. The new stand, whose King's Colour is shown here, was presented to the regiment in Corfu in October 1831 by Sir Alexander Woodford. As if to compensate for the poor showing of the painted colours, no expense was spared, and the new stand was richly embroidered. The centre bears the cipher of King William IV. As noted elsewhere, the inclusion of the Royal cipher was a feature common on King's Colours from around the turn of the 19th century, even though it was not included in the regulations. The Second Colour bore the simple regimental number in Arabic numerals in the centre. These colours were carried until 1847.

There was never any question of this incarnation of the 95th Foot taking over the battle honours won by its predecessor, since that regiment still existed as the un-numbered Rifle Brigade. Source: Milne, *Standards and Colours.*

H2: Regimental Colour, 55th (Westmoreland) Foot, 1850

The practice of including a distinctive badge as part of a battle honour was used only intermittently – Egypt (1801), India (1807), Hindoostan (1807) and Gibraltar (1836) were the only examples. The practice was revived for the campaign in China in 1842. In modern parlance, these are all 'theatre' honours, for service in a theatre of war rather than for a particular engagement.

The colour here was presented in 1850 and was carried during the Crimean War. The wreath is unusually richly embroidered. The Royal Colour bears the regimental number in Arabic numerals. Source: Milne, *Standards and Colours.*

H3: Regimental Colour, 14th (Buckinghamshire) Foot, 1876

This colour was very short-lived, part of a stand presented to the regiment by the Prince of Wales at Lucknow in January 1876. After the ceremony the Prince let it be known that he was so impressed by the bearing of the regiment that he intended to award it the subsidiary title of 'Prince of Wales's Own'. This was confirmed in the *London Gazette* of 6 June 1876. The new colours had therefore to be altered to include the new title. The centre now included the Prince of Wales's feathers and coronet above the regimental number; 'Buckinghamshire' was replaced by 'Prince of Wales's Own' in the centre, and relegated to a blue scroll placed across the bottom of the wreath.

The regiment is known to have received new colours in 1750, 1764, 1778, 1792, c.1809, 1819, 1835 and 1853. The badge of the Royal tiger and 'India' was granted on 8 November 1838 for services between 1808 and 1831. The white horse badge was granted by a special warrant dated 18 July 1873. The regiment had claimed that the white horse was a particular badge granted to them after performing guard duty at Windsor Castle and Hampton Court in 1765. From its wording, the letter included in the regimental history as supporting evidence appears irrelevant – no more than a general instruction about grenadier caps, sent out to the whole Army. Nevertheless, the regiment's officers used a white horse badge on their shako plates from 1820 onwards. The inset outline shows the reduced size of colours ordered in Queen's Regulations of 1868 – 36ins. by 45ins. – in proportion to the colour images. Sources: Public Record Office WO 32/6835; O'Donnell, H., *Historical Records of the 14th Regiment* (Devonport, c.1892).

H4: Regimental Colour, 1st Battalion, 24th (2nd Warwickshire) Foot, 1879

The 1/24th took only their Royal Colour into the field during the Zulu War; the Regimental Colour was left behind at the depot at Helpmakaar. When the defence line at the camp at Isandlwana was breached, Col. Pulleine ordered Lt. Melvill to secure the colour and prevent its capture. Trying to cross the Buffalo River on horseback, Melvill lost his seat and was washed down river, losing his grip on the flag. One of his brother officers, Lt. Coghill, turned back to help Melvill, but both were overwhelmed. In May, a patrol under Maj. Black of the 24th and Lt. Harford of the 99th found their bodies. Harford went a little further downstream, where he first found the colour case, and then the colour itself, wedged between some rocks. On 28 July 1880 the colour was shown to Queen Victoria, who placed a wreath of silver immortelles on the finial, and ordered that both colours should be adorned with such a wreath.

The colours of the 2/24th were also left behind in the camp at Isandlwana, but only one pole, case and finial was ever recovered. When a new stand was presented at Gibraltar in 1882 the relics were trooped as if they were whole.

Although it was not until 1881 that colours were last carried in action, it is apparent that their use was limited in a campaign like this. All three of the 24th's colours with the column were left in the tents in their cases rather than taken into the firing line. If they had been an essential feature of combat they would surely have accompanied the battalion into action. Another regiment in South Africa at this time, the 99th, also left their colours at a depot rather than take them into the field. Source: Atkinson, C.T., *The South Wales Borderers* (Brecon, 1937).

I1: Ensign, Wiltshire Militia, 1760

The details of the uniform are based upon a painting which hung in the officers' mess of the Wiltshire Regiment and shows the regiment drawn up on parade. Lawson, noting the presence of servants dressed in blue faced red, suggests that the combination of colours represented the livery colours of the Lord Lieutenant of Wiltshire, Lord Bruce. It may be significant in terms of the later history of this colour that the regimental facings were changed to yellow when Bruce retired and was replaced by Henry Herbert. Source: Lawson, C.C.P., *History of the Uniforms of the British Army* (London, 1961–66), vol.3.

I2: County Colour, Wiltshire Militia, 1760

The arms are those of the Lord Lieutenant of Wiltshire, Thomas Brudenell, Baron Bruce, which were granted in 1747. Source: Lawson, *History of the Uniforms of the British Army*, vol.3.

I3: Second Colour, Agbrigg Local Militia, 1808

This stand of colours was presented to the regiment upon its formation in 1808. The arms in the centre are those of Sir George Armytage Bt. The yellow sheet is unusual, since other local militia regiments in the West Riding of Yorkshire – the Claro, Craven, Sheffield, Staincross & Osgoldcross, Strafforth & Tickhill, Wakefield, West Halifax and York regiments – used dark green. The Agbrigg Local Militia incorporated men who had served with the Huddersfield Armed Association and the Huddersfield Fusiliers. The former was a legion-style unit; its infantry component carried a single colour, a Union Flag with the Royal arms in the centre, while the cavalry carried a crimson guidon. The Fusiliers also bore a King's Colour with the Royal arms in the centre. Their Second Colour was blue, with a central device depicting Britannia holding a shield inscribed *For God King and Country*, and accompanied by a lion. This central device is surrounded by a laurel wreath, entwined with a scroll bearing the unit's name. Source: Potter Berry, R., *A History of the Formation and Development of the Volunteer Infantry* (London, 1903).

J1: Second Colour, 1st British Fencibles, or Glengarry Regiment, 1803

Fencibles were just one element of the auxiliary forces raised to defend their country during the 18th and early 19th centuries. Fencible regiments were composed of volunteers who undertook to serve only within their own country (England or Scotland as the case may be) except in the case of invasion. Service in the Militia, on the other hand, was compulsory; while regiments of Volunteers undertook to serve only within their own county.

Fencible units were particularly popular in Scotland, where the militia had become moribund by 1745. Two units were raised during the Seven Years' War, three during the American War of Independence and 27 during the wars against France. All of the latter were disbanded at the Peace of Amiens.

Although the clan system was in decline as a social institution by this period, the traditional and sentimental influence of the great families was still important. The colour shown here has a centre badge of a clump of heath, a flower of the genus *Erica*, which was the plant badge of the McDonnells, the most prominent family in Glengarry. The stag's head crest of the Dukes of Gordon appears on the recruiting flag shown in a line illustration (and the family's plant badge of ivy became part of the regimental bonnet badge); the boar's head crest of the Campbell family became a badge on the colours of the 91st (Argyllshire) Foot in 1873; the motto of the Mackenzie family was used by the 78th Highlanders. Source: actual flag.

J2: Second Colour, Beverley Volunteers, 1808

The original Beverley Volunteers was formed in 1794, and was disbanded after the Peace of Amiens. It was reformed in 1803 at a strength of 150 men. The unit was disbanded in 1808, and replaced by the 3rd Regiment of East York Local Militia. The regiment wore red uniforms with blue facings, so its colour might be expected to reflect this; instead it is buff, following the facings of the East York Militia. (Another volunteer unit, the Hull and County Volunteers, also carried a buff colour, but in that case in keeping with their regimental facings.) The King's Colour was a plain Union flag with no decoration or inscription. In July 1804 the Minute Books of the Corporation record the decision that an *additional* colour bearing the arms of Beverley be presented to the Beverley Volunteers as a token of their public spirit and patriotic conduct 'at this important crisis in public affairs'. The use of the word 'additional' implies that a colour was already in use – perhaps the Union Flag. One local historian, writing in 1829, records that the colour cost some 70 guineas – an extraordinarily high sum and surely incorrect.

The colour of an Irish yeomanry regiment, the 3rd County of Dublin Brigade. Sheet: blue. Centre: red with yellow edges and lettering. Note the extraordinary rendering of the Union Flag in the canton, with an over-wide fimbration on the cross of St George, and a saltire that is far too narrow. Source: Hayes-McCoy, *Irish Flags.*

When the regiment was disbanded in 1808 the colours passed back into the hands of the Corporation. After the Reform Act they became the property of one of the commissioners responsible for the assets of the unreformed body, and his descendants deposited them in the local church. Sources: actual flag; Norfolk, R.W.S., *Militia, Yeomanry and Volunteer Forces of the East Riding 1689–1908* (York, 1965).

J3: Colour, Independent Tyreril Volunteers and Loyal Liney Volunteers, 1778

An unusual colour, belonging to a unit of volunteers from County Sligo, Ireland. In a list of volunteer units dated 1778 the Tyreril True Blues and the Liney Volunteers are listed as separate corps, but since they were raised in adjoining baronies (now spelt Tiraghrill and Leney) it is quite possible that the two small units amalgamated. The style of the basic colour is reminiscent of 17th century English patterns, or even those of contemporary Irish regiments in the French service. There is no evidence that the colour ever included a St Andrew's cross. Like the standards of their cavalry counterparts, the colours of the infantry regiments demonstrate that the Volunteer movement was not exclusively Protestant. Note here the use of specifically Catholic symbols such as the motto in Gaelic (*Laimh Ui hArigh* – possibly 'O'Hara's hand' although the exact significance of the words is now lost). The general pattern of this colour is similar to that of a Co. Tyrone unit, the Killymoon Battalion. The resemblance bears closer examination and suggests the possibility that some larger formation existed.

In contrast to the Volunteers, the Yeomanry movement of the early 19th century preferred to adopt colours that were closely modelled on British Regular Army practice. The harp, proudly borne by the Tyreril Volunteers and many others, had become tainted as a symbol after its use by the rebels of 1798; so the devices adopted by the more narrowly Protestant Yeomanry movement placed strong emphasis on the imperial crown in place of the Irish crown, the Union canton and the Union wreath. Source: Hayes-McCoy, *Irish Flags*.

J4: Regimental Colour, Robin Hood Rifles, 1859

The regiments of rifle volunteers, created in 1859–60 in response to a perceived French threat, were specifically denied colours by the terms of the Volunteer Regulations. However, local pride dictated that some kind of flag should be presented, and many units received 'colours', 'flags' or 'banners'. Like those of the Volunteers of the Napoleonic period, these flags showed little evidence of obedience to regulation of any kind. The colours of the Robin Hood Rifles (more officially, 1st Nottinghamshire Volunteer Rifle Corps) were presented to the Corps on the Trent Bridge Cricket Ground on 3 October 1860. The use of dark green and black recalls the traditional colours of rifle corps uniforms. The badge in the centre was that of the Corps; in the lower hoist corner is a shield with the arms of the city of Nottingham. The 'King's Colour' was a plain Union Flag with a fringe. Source: Iliffe, R. & Baguley, W., *The Robin Hood Rifles 1837–1901* (Nottingham, 1975); further information from the Regimental Museum.

INDEX

Figures in **bold** refer to illustrations

COMPANION SERIES FROM OSPREY

ESSENTIAL HISTORIES
Concise studies of the motives, methods and repercussions of human conflict, spanning history from ancient times to the present day. Each volume studies one major war or arena of war, providing an indispensable guide to the fighting itself, the people involved, and its lasting impact on the world around it.

CAMPAIGN
Accounts of history's greatest conflicts, detailing the command strategies, tactics, movements and actions of the opposing forces throughout the crucial stages of each campaign. Full-colour battle scenes, 3-dimensional 'bird's-eye views', photographs and battle maps guide the reader through each engagement from its origins to its conclusion.

ORDER OF BATTLE
The greatest battles in history, featuring unit-by-unit examinations of the troops and their movements as well as analysis of the commanders' original objectives and actual achievements.Colour maps including a large fold-out base map, organizational diagrams and photographs help the reader to trace the course of the fighting in unprecedented detail.

MEN-AT-ARMS
The uniforms, equipment, insignia, history and organisation of the world's military forces from earliest times to the present day. Authoritative text and full-colour artwork, photographs and diagrams bring over 5000 years of history vividly to life.

NEW VANGUARD
The design, development, operation and history of the machinery of warfare through the ages. Photographs, full-colour artwork and cutaway drawings support detailed examinations of the most significant mechanical innovations in the history of human conflict.

WARRIOR
Insights into the daily lives of history's fighting men and women, past and present, detailing their motivation, training, tactics, weaponry and experiences. Meticulously researched narrative and full-colour artwork, photographs, and scenes of battle and daily life provide detailed accounts of the experiences of combatants through the ages.

AIRCRAFT OF THE ACES
Portraits of the elite pilots of the 20th century's major air campaigns, including unique interviews with surviving aces. Unit listings, scale plans and full-colour artwork combine with the best archival photography available to provide a detailed insight into the experience of war in the air.

COMBAT AIRCRAFT
The world's greatest military aircraft and combat units and their crews, examined in detail. Each exploration of the leading technology, men and machines of aviation history is supported by unit listings and other data, artwork, scale plans, and archival photography.